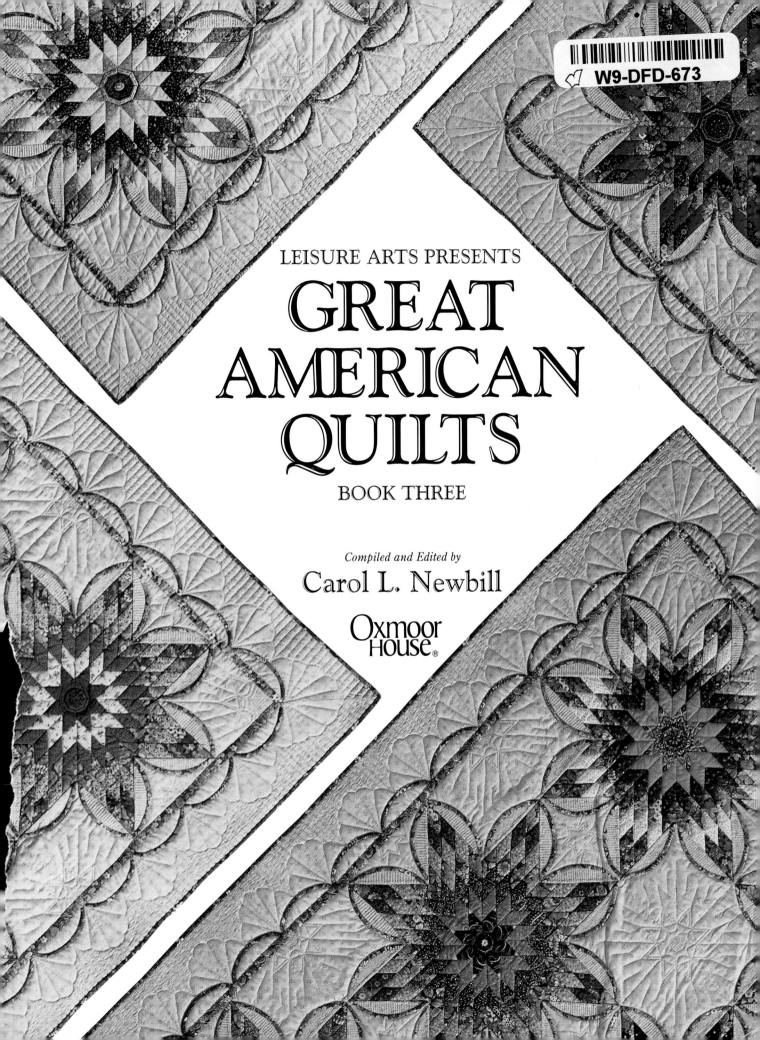

LEISURE ARTS PRESENTS

GREAT AMERICAN QUILTS

BOOK THREE

Compiled and Edited by

Carol L. Newbill

Oxmoor
House.

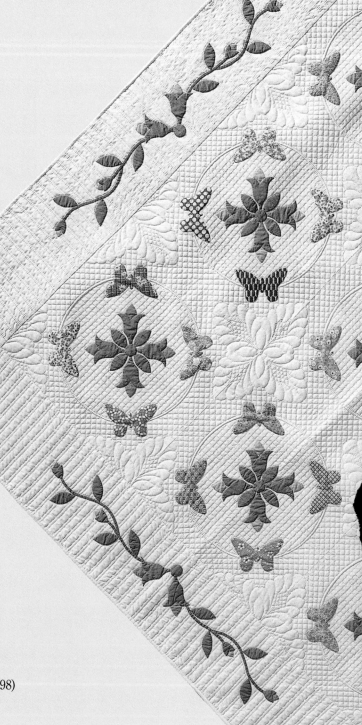

©1995 by Oxmoor House, Inc.
Book Division of Southern Progress Corporation
P.O. Box 2463, Birmingham, AL 35201

Published by Oxmoor House, Inc., and Leisure Arts, Inc.

Library of Congress Catalog Card Number: 86-62283
ISBN: 0-8487-1461-X
ISSN: 1076-7673
Manufactured in the United States of America
First Printing 1995

Editor-in-Chief: Nancy Fitzpatrick Wyatt
Senior Crafts Editor:
    Susan Ramey Cleveland
Senior Editor, Editorial Services:
    Olivia Kindig Wells
Art Director: James Boone

Great American Quilts Book Three

Editor: Carol Logan Newbill
Editorial Assistant: Adrienne E. Short
Copy Editor: Susan S. Cheatham
Production and Distribution Director: Phillip Lee
Production Manager: Gail H. Morris
Associate Production Manager: Theresa L. Beste
Production Assistant: Marianne Jordan
Designer: Eleanor Cameron
Patterns and Illustrations: Kelly Davis
Publishing Systems Administrator: Rick Tucker
Senior Photographer: John O'Hagan
Photo Stylist: Katie Stoddard

Cover Quilt: *Stars with Flaire*, by Christine Kennedy (page 98)

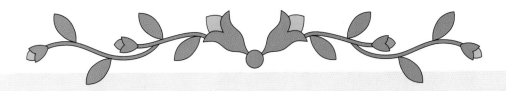

EDITOR'S NOTE

Small quilts, wall quilts, challenge quilts, scrap quilts: Quilters love making all sorts of quilts. For this year's special chapter, we have chosen six stunning quilts made from ordinary shapes—squares, triangles, hexagons—to bring you "Simple Pleasures." Look at Sammie Simpson's *Fine Feathered Friend* and Doris Dunlap's *Converging Triangles* to see how two very different quilters handled designs made from triangles. For those of you who enjoy challenges, see how well Marybeth Cieplinski handled the challenge of making a very small quilt, 28" square, in only three colors in her *Cosmic Explosion*. And for an old-fashioned scrap quilt made from a seldom-seen pattern, see Marianna Frost's *Memory Chain*.

Chickens, anyone? Take a look at Freddy Moran's spunky, scrappy *Funky Chicken* that leads off "Quilts Across America"—and find out why Freddy spent several months afraid to open her mail! Also included in this chapter are angels and a quilt with lots of finny, Finnish fish.

Cactus blossoms, stars, butterflies, and fans are among the beautiful designs that round out this year's collection of 28 quilts. So whether you prefer quilts with "Traditions" or those that are "Simple Pleasures," you're sure to find something to please.

Mystery fans, take note! Somewhere in this book is a quilt hiding two gray cats. When you find the cats, write us at the address below and tell us the name of the quilt and the page number. (Don't forget to include your name, address, and telephone number.) If you are one of the first 50 with the correct answer, you'll win a small prize!

Where do our Great American quilters come from? They come from Connecticut and California, from Minnesota and Alabama, from Wisconsin and from Florida. This year's book features quilts from quilters and quilting groups in 17 different states across America.

If your state isn't represented, let us put a star on next year's map for you! For information on submitting a quilt, write to *Great American Quilts* Editor, Oxmoor House, 2100 Lakeshore Drive, Birmingham, AL 35209.

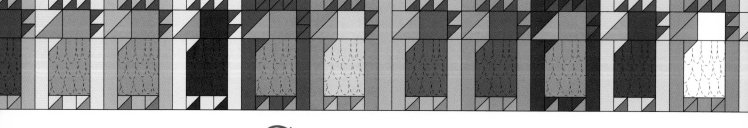

CONTENTS
EDITOR'S NOTE 3

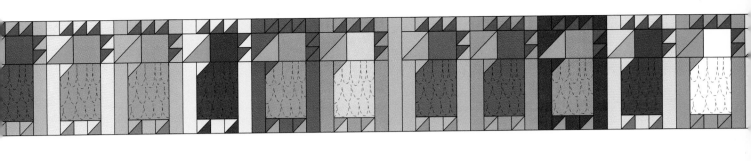

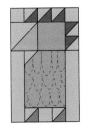

SIMPLE PLEASURES

"Some people get so worried about what color goes with what that they forget to just trust their eye. If you like how it looks, use it!"

Kathy Munkelwitz
ISLE, MINNESOTA

Farmer and quiltmaker Kathy Munkelwitz lives with her husband, Alton, near Lake Mille Lacs, about 100 miles north of Minneapolis. The nearest quilt shop is 50 miles away! But Kathy loves fabric and depends on each season's new lines to spark ideas for her quilts. So what does a country quilter do? Opens her own shop, of course!

During the summer months, Kathy and two of her daughters operate Kathy's Quilts and Crafts Shop in an old house that once was a trading post in the nearby town of Wahkon. From Memorial Day through Thanksgiving, Kathy works two days a week at the shop and spends the rest of the week making quilts for sale while her daughters tend the shop. She also makes a number of commissioned pieces and makes one quilt for competition each year.

"The feedback from my quilts is so gratifying," Kathy says. "I even get 'thank you' letters from people who receive my quilts as gifts." And though she has won many awards in competition, the Viewers' Choice awards are those that mean the most to her.

Table Scraps
1993

Kathy likes to use dark colors and plaids in her quilt projects. She often buys fabric without a specific project in mind, resulting in lots of scraps after several small pieces are completed. "I went into my studio one day," Kathy says, "and all these scraps were stacked on my cutting table waiting to be put away. They looked so pretty together that I decided to make a quilt using only those scraps on my table—truly a 'table scrap' quilt!"

Kathy had seen a quilt using the asymmetrical star pattern and decided she would like to try it. "So the quilt just developed," she says. "I placed the stars every which way and then filled in the gaps with irregular pieces and several small star blocks." She continued the "every which way" theme in the quilting, using many different quilting patterns over the body of the quilt. "It was lots of fun!" she says.

Table Scraps won first place in scrap quilts at the 1993 Minnesota State Fair. And in 1994, Kathy took home both the Judge's Choice and Viewers' Choice ribbons for *Table Scraps* from the Minnesota Quilters Guild show.

Table Scraps

Finished Quilt Size
93" x 103"

Number of Blocks and Finished Size
15 Block 1   12" x 12"
8 Block 2   6" x 6"

Fabric Requirements
Navy   3 yards*
Brown print   2¼ yards
Dark scraps   6 yards
Backing   8½ yards

*Use fabric remaining after cutting borders for bias binding.

Pieces to Cut
Navy
   2 (4" x 103½") outer border strips
   2 (4" x 86") outer border strips
   2 (3½" x 90½") inner border strips
   2 (3½" x 68") inner border strips
Brown print
   90 A
   60 B
   30 C
   60 D
   30 F
   64 G
Dark scraps**
   826 A
   23 F
   54 (2" x 3½") strips
   52 (2" x 6½") strips
   52 (2" x 9½") strips
   74 (2" x 12½") strips
   2 (2" x 15½") strips

**For each Block 1, cut 4 Bs and 4 Es from 1 scrap fabric and 6 As and 1 F from second scrap fabric.

Quilt Top Assembly
1. Referring to *Block 1 Assembly Diagram,* join 6 brown print As, 6 scrap As, 4 brown print Bs, 4 scrap Bs, 2 brown print Cs, 4 brown print Ds, 4 scrap Es, 2 brown print Fs, and 1 scrap F as shown to complete 1 Block 1. Repeat to make 11 Block 1s.

2. Referring to *Partial Block 1 Assembly Diagram,* join 4 brown print As, 4 scrap As, 2 brown print Bs, 2 scrap Bs, 1 brown print C, 4 brown print Ds, 4 scrap Es, 2 brown print Fs, and 1 scrap F as shown to complete 1 Unit I. Repeat to make 4 Unit Is.

To make 1 Unit II, join 2 brown print As, 2 scrap As, 2 brown print Bs, 2 scrap Bs, and 1 brown print C as shown in *Partial Block 1 Assembly Diagram.* Repeat to make 4 Unit IIs.

3. Referring to *Block 2 Assembly Diagram,* join 8 scrap As, 4 scrap Bs, and 8 brown print Gs as shown to complete 1 Block 2. Repeat to make 8 Block 2s.

4. Join 216 scrap As into 53 four-patch units and 2 two-patch units. (See *Partial Block 1 Assembly Diagram,* Unit II, for example of four-patch unit made from 4 As.)

5. Referring to *Quilt Top Assembly Diagram,* join blocks, strips, two-patch and four-patch units, and remaining Fs in rows as follows:

Row 1: 1 Block 2, 8 four-patch units, 1 F, 10 (2" x 3½") strips, 6 (2" x 6½") strips, 4 (2" x 9½") strips, 8 (2" x 12½") strips.

Row 2: 2 Block 1s, 1 Block 1 Unit I, 1 Block 2, 3 four-patch units, 2 Fs, 2 (2" x 3½") strips, 2 (2" x 6½") strips, 8 (2" x 9½") strips, 12 (2" x 12½") strips.

Row 3: 2 Block 1s, 1 Block 1 Unit I, 1 Block 1 Unit II, 1 Block 2, 7 four-patch units, 2 Fs, 18 (2" x 3½") strips, 4 (2" x 6½") strips, 8 (2" x 9½") strips, 12 (2" x 12½") strips, 2 (2" x 15½") strips.

Row 4: 2 Block 1s, 1 Block 1 Unit I, 1 Block 1 Unit II, 1 Block 2, 2 two-patch units, 12 four-patch units, 1 F, 6 (2" x 3½") strips, 12 (2" x 6½") strips, 12 (2" x 9½") strips, 8 (2" x 12½") strips.

Row 5: 2 Block 1s, 1 Block 1 Unit I, 1 Block 1 Unit II, 2 Block 2s, 9 four-patch units, 1 F, 4 (2" x 3½") strips, 12 (2" x 6½") strips, 10 (2" x 9½") strips, 10 (2" x 12½") strips.

Row 6: 3 Block 1s, 1 Block 1 Unit II, 2 Block 2s, 15 four-patch units, 1 F, 14 (2" x 3½") strips, 16 (2" x 6½") strips, 12 (2" x 9½") strips, 22 (2" x 12½") strips.

6. Join rows. Join 3½" x 68" navy inner borders to top and bottom of quilt. Join 3½" x 90½" navy inner borders to sides of quilt, butting corners.

7. To make top pieced border, join 100 scrap As into 2 rows of 50 each; join rows as shown in *Quilt Top Assembly Diagram.* Repeat to make bottom border. Join to top and bottom of quilt. To make 1 side pieced border, join 128 scrap As into 2 rows of 64 each; join rows as above. Repeat to make second side pieced border. Join to sides of quilt, butting corners.

8. Join 4" x 86" navy outer borders to top and bottom of quilt. Join 4" x 103½" navy outer borders to sides of quilt, butting corners.

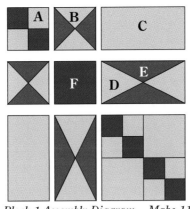

Block 1 Assembly Diagram—Make 11.

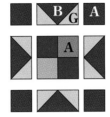

Block 2 Assembly Diagram—Make 8.

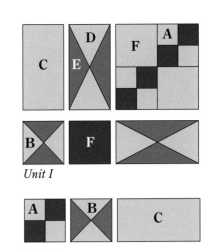

Unit I

Unit II

Partial Block 1 Assembly Diagram —Make 4 Unit Is and 4 Unit IIs.

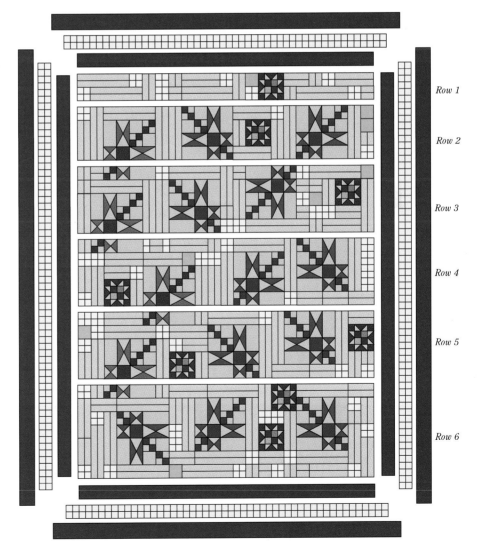

Row 1

Row 2

Row 3

Row 4

Row 5

Row 6

Quilt Top Assembly Diagram

11

Quilting

Quilt pieced area in-the-ditch or as desired. Quilt *Rope Quilting Pattern* in inner navy border. Quilt *Arch Quilting Pattern* in outer navy border.

Finished Edges

Bind with bias binding made from navy.

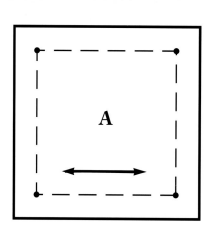

A

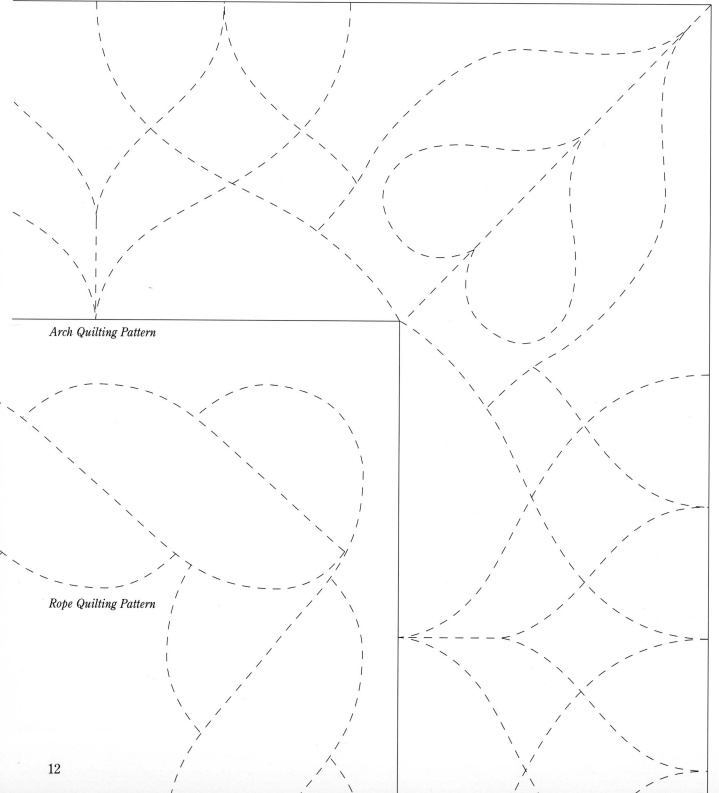

Arch Quilting Pattern

Rope Quilting Pattern

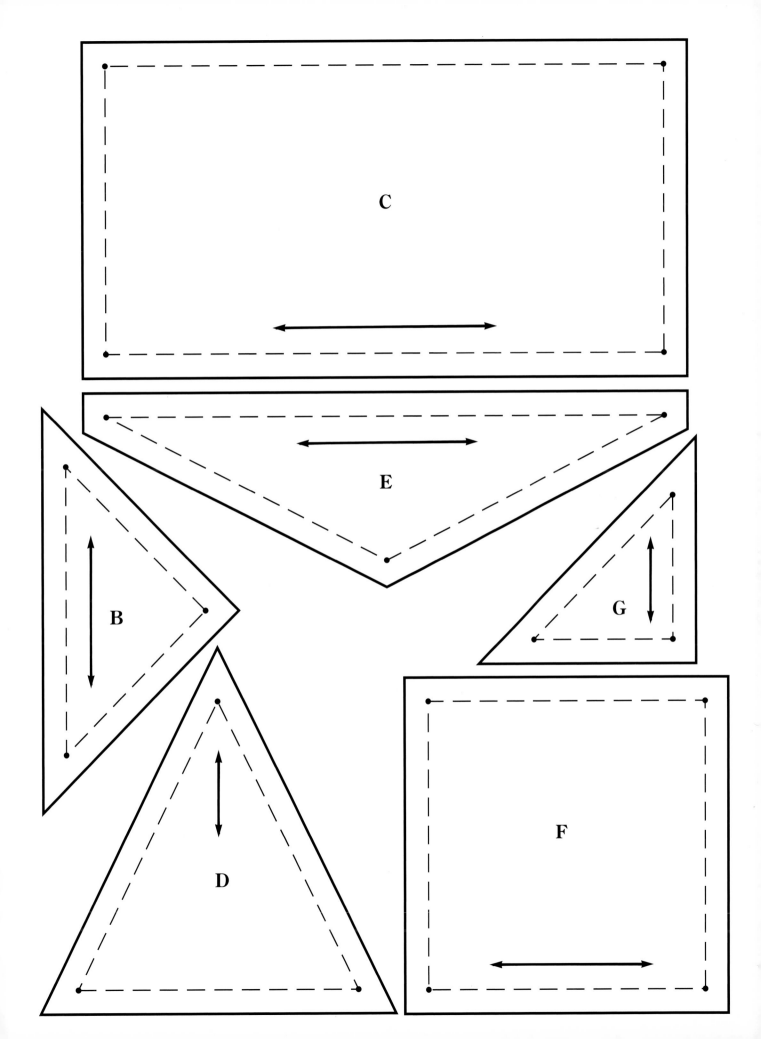

"When people ask what I do for a living, I say I'm a quilter."

Marybeth E. Cieplinski
KENT, OHIO

Marybeth fell in love with quilts about 15 years ago, when she bought a quilting magazine. Teaching herself English piecing from the magazine was her first step, and she spent three years simply piecing tops before beginning to quilt them. "I like the piecing process best," Marybeth says. "Once it's pieced, I consider the quilt to be done, because I can see my design as a whole." In spite of her preference, Marybeth handquilts a number of projects each year. "I like miniature and wall quilts best," she says, "but I've just finished the largest quilt I've ever done, piecing and quilting it all by hand. My younger son is using it on his bed this winter."

Like many quiltmakers, Marybeth makes quilts and exhibits them simply for her own satisfaction. "I knew I had finally convinced my husband that I was serious about this craft when he began wrapping my Christmas presents in fabric," she says. "And for my 40th birthday, he gave me 40 yards of fabric—one yard every day for the 40 days beforehand. When people ask what I do for a living, I say I'm a quilter. I can't imagine doing anything else."

Cosmic Explosion
1993

Cosmic Explosion is Marybeth's answer to a challenge posed by her guild, the Portage Patchers of Mogadore, Ohio. The piece had to be a small wall hanging, using only black, white or gray, and up to ¼ yard of one other color. Marybeth not only accepted this challenge, but set herself a further goal.

"I wanted to push myself to do something that frightened me," she says. "Piecing 1" squares was very scary."

After designing and piecing the top, Marybeth, pleased with the effect of the red exploding outward from the center, chose an appropriate name for the quilt. "I'd like to do a full-sized version of this design," she says, "but I hate making the same thing twice." With her design ability and her tendency to push herself in new directions, we're betting Marybeth has a large version of *Cosmic Explosion* to share with us in the near future!

Cosmic Explosion

Finished Quilt Size
28" x 28"

Fabric Requirements

White	1 yard
Red	¼ yard
Black	½ yard
Backing	1 yard
Black for bias binding	½ yard

Pieces to Cut
White
  4 (1½" x 26½") outer border strips
  2 (1½" x 18½") inner border strips
  2 (1½" x 16½") inner border strips
  48 A
  44 B
  56 C
Red
  28 A
  8 C
  8 D
Black
  92 A
  24 B
  24 C
  20 D
  5 E

Quilt Top Assembly

1. Referring to *Assembly Diagram 1*, join As, Bs, Cs, Ds, and Es in units as shown. Join units into rows; join rows to complete center of quilt. Join 1½" x 16½" white border strips to top and bottom of quilt center. Join 1½" x 18½" white border strips to sides of quilt, butting corners.

2. Referring to *Assembly Diagram 2*, join As, Bs, Cs, and Ds in units as shown. Join 5 units at top of quilt into top border; repeat to join 5 units at bottom into bottom border. Join to top and bottom of quilt. Join remaining units into side borders as shown; join to sides of quilt.

3. Referring to *Assembly Diagram 3*, join As, Bs, Cs, and Ds in units as shown. Join 7 units at top of quilt into top border; repeat to join 7 units at bottom of quilt. Join to top and bottom of quilt. Join remaining units into side borders as shown; join to sides of quilt.

4. Join 2 (1½" x 26½") white border strips to top and bottom of quilt. Join 1 red A to each end of remaining border strips as shown; join to sides of quilt, butting corners.

Quilting
Quilt in-the-ditch around borders and units, as shown in *Quilting Diagram*. Quilt diagonal lines from corners toward center as shown.

Finished Edges
Bind with bias binding made from black.

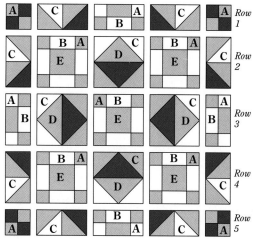

Assembly Diagram 1

Assembly Diagram 2

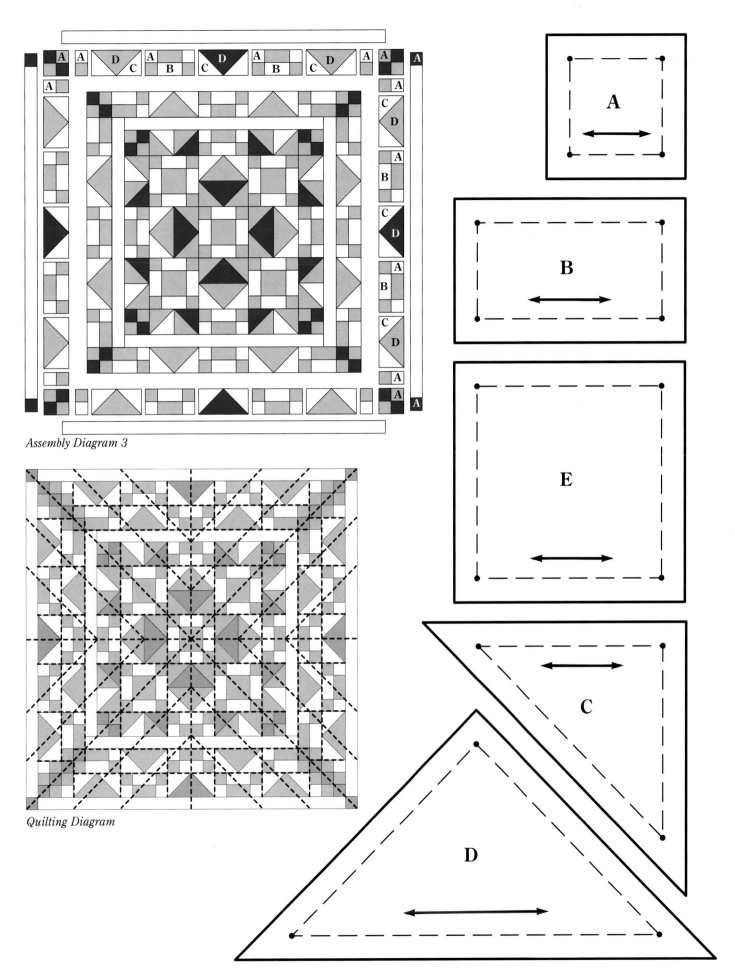

Assembly Diagram 3

Quilting Diagram

A

B

E

C

D

"I like traditional patterns with a contemporary approach—like this Flower Garden done my way."

Regina Smythe
MOUNT VERNON, OHIO

"I may be the only quilter in the United States who has pictures of her quilts projected at a Grateful Dead concert," says Regina Smythe with a smile.

Although Regina, a native of Lancaster County, Pennsylvania, grew up surrounded by colorful quilts, she didn't begin making them herself until 1985. A visit to a quilt show in Gatlinburg, Tennessee, led her to take a course at the local vocational school. "That was all it took," says Regina. "I quickly became a quiltaholic."

Regina enjoys working with traditional patterns, giving them a personal, contemporary twist and using her favorite bright colors. "My husband says he can date my quilts by their progression from neutrals to brights," she says. "I like working with exciting patterns and increasing the contrast in each new quilt."

Regina finds that her son Bill, a professional photographer, is a constant source of ideas and a good critic of color. "He's also my rock connection," she explains. "He takes the color slides that are projected as part of the concert light show." It's quite a compliment to Regina's sense of color that her quilts are lively enough to hold their own with the Grateful Dead!

My Flower Garden
1994

"A friend of mine is a painter," Regina says. "When I saw some of her paintings of flowers, I wanted to make my own flower garden." Because she likes to hand-piece and enjoys working with traditional patterns, Regina chose to use the Grandmother's Flower Garden pattern for her own garden.

"It took a while for me to think of arranging the flowers this way," she says. "I enjoyed making the flowers from so many happy colors, but I didn't want to set them in the traditional way."

Regina is still experimenting with the Flower Garden pattern. In addition to *My Flower Garden,* she has completed a wall hanging with red and yellow flowers, and is planning still others. "As I go to more shows and museums, I realize how many new ideas and color schemes I have to experiment with," she says. "I'll never run out of ideas for new quilts."

My Flower Garden

Finished Quilt Size
55" x 74"

Number of Blocks and Finished Size
135 flower units   4¾" diameter

Fabric Requirements

Dark red	2¼ yards*
Pink	2 yards
Dark yellow scraps	½ yard
Light yellow scraps	1½ yards
Dark red scraps	½ yard
Light red scraps	1½ yards
Dark blue-green scraps	½ yard
Light blue-green scraps	1½ yards
Dark green scraps	½ yard
Backing	4¾ yards

*Use fabric remaining after cutting borders for bias binding.

Pieces to Cut
Dark red
  2 (5½" x 74½") outer border strips
  2 (5½" x 55½") outer border strips
Pink
  2 (1¼" x 64½") inner border strips
  2 (1¼" x 45½") inner border strips

Quilt Top Assembly
1. From scraps, cut 6 light hexagons from same fabric plus 1 dark hexagon for each flower unit (45 dark and 270 light hexagons of each color group). Referring to *Flower Unit Assembly Diagram*, join 6 light hexagons to 1 dark hexagon to make 1 flower unit. Make 45 yellow flower units, 45 red flower units, and 45 blue-green flower units for a total of 135 flower units. For help in piecing hexagons, see "Hand Piecing" on page 140.

2. From scraps, cut additional hexagons as follows: 4 dark yellow, 38 light yellow, 2 dark red, 20 light red, 3 dark blue-green, 52 light blue-green, 86 dark green.

3. On a floor or design wall, arrange flower units in color groups as shown in photograph to make a rectangle approximately 49" x 70". Use hexagons cut in Step 2 to fill areas between flower units. When satisfied with arrangement, join units and hexagons. Trim rectangle to 45½" x 64½".

4. Join 1¼" x 45½" pink inner border strips to top and bottom of quilt. Join 1¼" x 64½" pink inner border strips to sides of quilt, mitering corners.

5. Join 5½" x 55½" dark red outer border strips to top and bottom of quilt. Join 5½" x 74½" dark red outer border strips to sides of quilt, mitering corners.

Quilting

Quilt central hexagon, outside edge of each flower unit, and pink inner border in-the-ditch. Quilt *Daisy Quilting Pattern* in dark red outer border.

Finished Edges

Bind with bias binding made from dark red.

Daisy Quilting Pattern

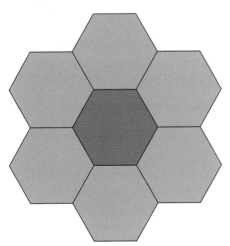

Flower Unit Assembly Diagram

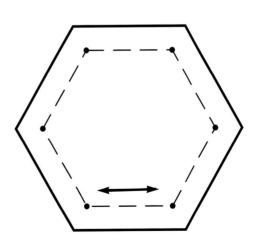

Doris Angell Dunlap
SAGINAW, MICHIGAN

"I like to create my own quilting designs," says Doris Dunlap. "They're everywhere—from antique china and glass to the back of a store-bought cookie."

As a child, Doris helped her grandmother cut out hexagons for quilts, but she didn't really begin quilting until 1976, when she took an adult education class. Since that time, she has made many quilts and wall hangings for family and friends. "I like making traditional or Amish-style quilts," she says. "Sometimes I'll make traditional patterns with some changes."

Although Doris's quilts have won a number of awards and several have been published, Doris does not consider herself a professional quiltmaker. "Quilting has been a great satisfaction to me," she says. "Through quilting, I've met many people whom I would not otherwise have had a chance to know. And although I enjoy the praise from my family and friends, I know that in years to come, my quilts will be a tangible remembrance that I once was here."

Converging Triangles
1984

"I love scrap quilts," Doris says, "and I like most of the triangle arrangements I've seen." Her preferences are evident in *Converging Triangles,* a complex-looking quilt that is really very simple to make.

Doris saw a similar quilt at a local show but did not like the fact that the quilt was square. After drafting a rectangular version of the design, she was delighted to discover the illusion of curves in a top pieced entirely of straight lines. "The border required a geometric design," Doris says, "so I doodled awhile before I came up with the triangular quilting pattern."

Converging Triangles has appeared at several local and regional shows and won a second-place ribbon in the 1988 Mt. Clemens Great Lakes Quilt Show.

Quilt Top Assembly

1. Referring to *Unit Assembly Diagram* and *Quilt Top Assembly Diagram*, join triangles into 8 units, alternating light and dark as shown. Note that 4 units will have a light triangle at the point and 4 will have a dark triangle.

2. Arrange units as shown in *Quilt Top Assembly Diagram*. Join units in groups of 4; join groups. Trim outside edges of quilt top as shown in *Unit Assembly Diagram* to form a 68½" x 88½" rectangle.

3. Join 6½" x 80½" blue borders to top and bottom of quilt. Join 6½" x 100½" blue borders to sides of quilt, mitering corners.

Quilting

Quilt triangles in-the-ditch or as desired. Quilt ½" diagonal lines in blue borders.

Finished Edges

Bind with bias binding made from blue.

Converging Triangles

Finished Quilt Size
80" x 100"

Fabric Requirements

Blue	3¼ yards*
Light scraps	3½ yards
Dark scraps	3¼ yards
Backing	7½ yards

*Use fabric remaining after cutting borders for bias binding.

Pieces to Cut
Blue
   2 (6½" x 100½") border strips
   2 (6½" x 80½") border strips
Light scraps
   334 triangles
Dark scraps
   318 triangles

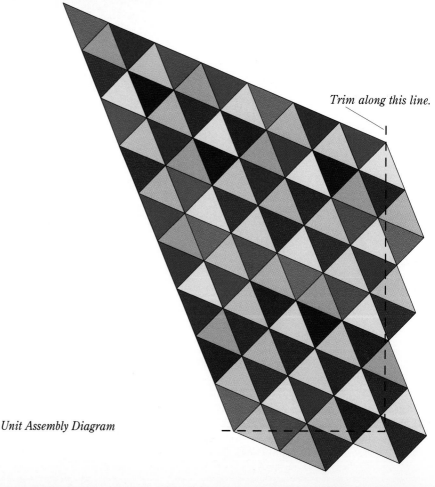

Trim along this line.

Unit Assembly Diagram

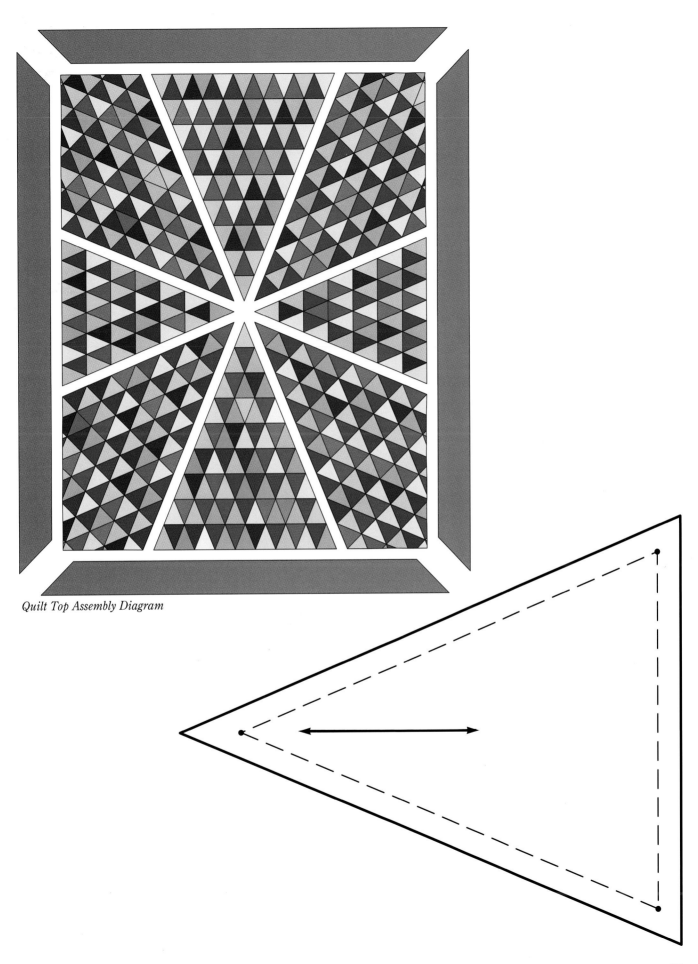

Quilt Top Assembly Diagram

"I have so many quilts in so many stages of completion—I guess 'Quilt in Progress' must be my favorite step!"

Marianna Frost
CALVERT, TEXAS

Although no one in her family was a quilter, Marianna Frost taught herself to quilt at age 13 by making a crazy quilt from her father's wide silk neckties. "I hand-pieced it and feather-stitched over all the seams," she says, "and I've been learning ever since." Now a quilt teacher certified by the National Quilting Association, Marianna lectures and writes for quilting magazines while she continues to make quilts.

As the only quiltmaker in the family, she has inherited the Frost quilting frame brought across the Appalachians by covered wagon 220 years ago. "My husband, Ken, thinks he's been sleeping in a canopy bed," she says, "because the frame has been hanging over the bed for most of the 40 years we've been married!"

Ask her which part of quilting is her favorite step, and Marianna answers, "I have so many quilts in so many stages of completion—I guess 'Quilt in Progress' must be my favorite step!"

Memory Chain
1993

Memory Chain is Marianna's adaptation of a traditional pattern she has had since the 1960s. The quilt is made using her favorite scrap technique. "I have dozens of scrap quilts in progress at any one time, each in its own plastic bag," Marianna says. "Any fabric scrap larger than a fingernail and smaller than half a yard is cut and distributed among as many bags as possible. I have tiny bags of miniature pieces and jumbo bags exploding at the seams waiting to be made into bed quilts. Every so often, I sit down and sew all the pieces together."

To unify the scraps, Marianna chose a print of teddy bears on a green background, once a set of curtains, to use for the repeating squares on point. "The colors are *not* placed randomly," she says. "I try to place each fabric next to a piece with a similar or complementary color. Then I always use a lot of red for drama and pizzazz!"

Memory Chain

Finished Quilt Size
73" x 88½"

**Number of Blocks and
Finished Size**
90 blocks 7½" x 7½"

Fabric Requirements
Green 2¾ yards*
Muslin 3½ yards
Dark print ¾ yard**
Light and
  medium scraps 3¾ yards
Backing 5½ yards

*Use fabric remaining after cutting borders for bias binding.
**Marianna chose a conversation print and centered the motifs in each A.

Pieces to Cut
Green
  2 (3½" x 89") border strips
  2 (3½" x 74") border strips
Muslin
  198 B
  180 D
  18 E
  18 E rev.

Dark print
  45 A
Light and medium scraps
  414 B
  594 C

Quilt Top Assembly

1. Referring to *Block 1 Assembly Diagram,* join 1 dark print A, 4 muslin Bs, 4 scrap Bs, 4 scrap Cs, and 2 muslin Ds as shown to complete 1 Block 1. Repeat to make 45 Block 1s.

Referring to *Half-Block 1 Assembly Diagram,* join 2 muslin Bs, 4 scrap Bs, 2 scrap Cs, 1 muslin E, and 1 muslin E rev. as shown to complete 1 Half-Block 1. Repeat to make 9 Half-Block 1s.

Referring to *Block 2 Assembly Diagram,* join 4 scrap Bs, 8 scrap Cs, and 2 muslin Ds as shown to complete 1 Block 2. Repeat to make 45 Block 2s.

Referring to *Half-Block 2 Assembly Diagram,* join 2 scrap Bs, 4 scrap Cs, 1 muslin E, and 1 muslin E rev. as shown to complete 1 Half-Block 2. Repeat to make 9 Half-Block 2s.

2. Referring to *Quilt Top Assembly Diagram,* join 4 Half-Block 1s and 5 Half-Block 2s for Row 1, beginning with Half-Block 2 and alternating half-blocks. In same manner, join 5 Half-Block 1s and 4 Half-Block 2s for Row 12, beginning with Half-Block 1 and alternating half-blocks.

For rows 2, 4, 6, 8, and 10, join 5 Block 1s and 4 Block 2s, beginning with Block 1 and alternating blocks. For remaining rows, join 4 Block 1s and 5 Block 2s, beginning with Block 2. Join rows as shown in *Quilt Top Assembly Diagram.*

3. Join 3½" x 74" green borders to top and bottom of quilt. Join 3½" x 89" green borders to sides of quilt, mitering corners.

Quilting
Quilt in-the-ditch or as desired.

Finished Edges
Bind with bias binding made from green.

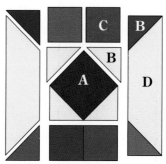
Block 1 Assembly Diagram—Make 45.

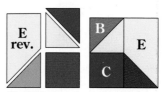
Half-Block 1 Assembly Diagram—Make 9.

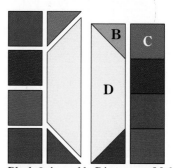
Block 2 Assembly Diagram—Make 45.

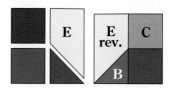
Half-Block 2 Assembly Diagram—Make 9.

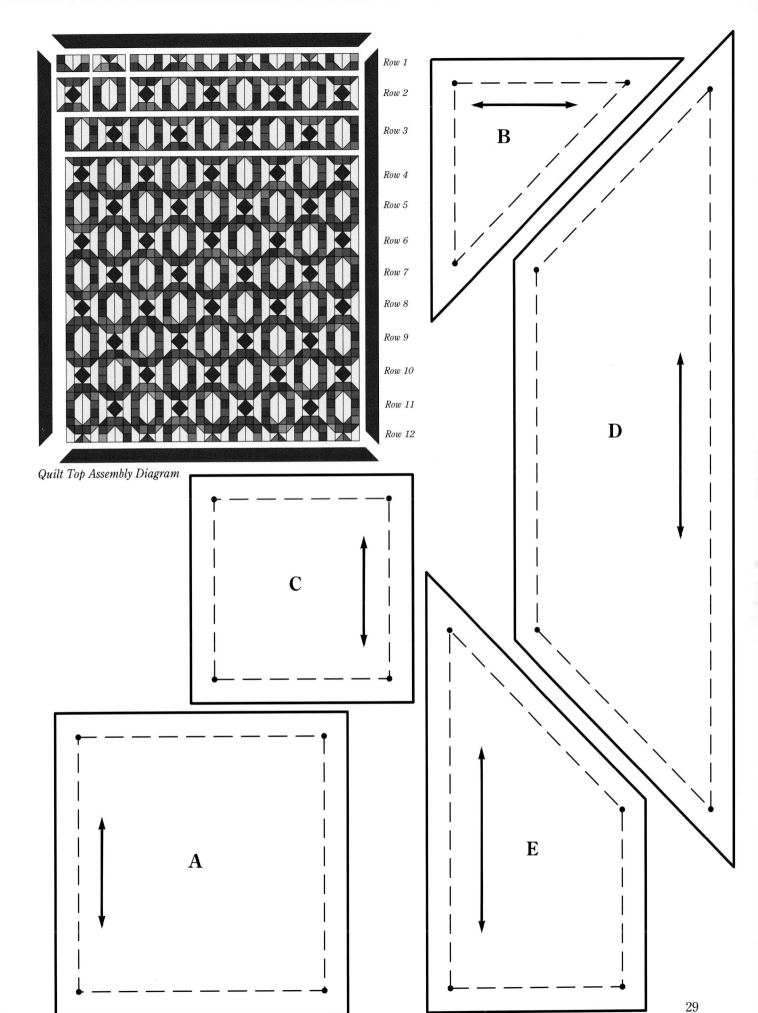

Quilt Top Assembly Diagram

Row 1
Row 2
Row 3
Row 4
Row 5
Row 6
Row 7
Row 8
Row 9
Row 10
Row 11
Row 12

B

D

C

A

E

29

Sammie Simpson
ALPHARETTA, GEORGIA

If the quiltmakers of America ever held a Quilting Olympics, Sammie Simpson would certainly be a favorite for the gold medal in machine quilting.

"I've only been quilting since 1983," Sammie says. "I started out hand quilting all of my pieces and really looked down my nose at machine quilting. Then I realized that I had too much fabric and too little time to hand-quilt all the things I wanted to do, so I just kept on practicing. Now I'm teaching machine quilting!"

That can-do attitude is a hallmark of this energetic quilter. In just 12 years, she has completed more than 100 quilts and won many awards at both the state and national levels. In 1994, Sammie was awarded a high-profile commission from the Atlanta Committee for the Olympic Games. She was chosen to quilt *A Quilt of Leaves,* the official "Look of the Games" conceived by a national design team and made by Barbara Abrelat of Decatur, Georgia, for the Centennial Olympics to be held in Atlanta in 1996.

Fine Feathered Friend
1994

Fine Feathered Friend is just one of the 400 quilts made by Georgia quilters in celebration of the 1996 Summer Olympic Games. One quilt will be presented to the flag bearer of each participating country, and another will be given to each nation's Olympic organizing committee.

The center medallion of *Fine Feathered Friend* consists of a Martha Washington's Star surrounded by Sammie's version of Trip Around the World. In each corner is a Friendship Star surrounded by Ocean Waves.

"The quilt really named itself," Sammie says. "I was trying to convey to those athletes who will be our guests here that we offer our friendship to all countries."

Fine Feathered Friend

Finished Quilt Size
52" x 68"

Fabric Requirements
Muslin	4¼ yards
Red prints	⅛ yard
Dark prints	¾ yard
Light prints	1¼ yards
Muslin for backing	3¼ yards
Navy for bias binding	1 yard

Pieces to Cut
Muslin
- 2 (19¼") squares*
- 2 (3¼") squares**
- 2 (10½" x 28½") E
- 2 (12½" x 18½") F
- 428 B

Red prints
- 20 B

Dark prints
- 4 A
- 228 B

Light prints
- 120 B

*Cut in half diagonally for 4 D.
**Cut in half diagonally for 4 C.

Quilt Top Assembly
1. Referring to *Quilt Top Assembly Diagram*, join 136 muslin Bs, 44 light print Bs, 64 dark print Bs, and 4 red print Bs as shown to make central diamond. Join muslin Cs to corners of diamond to complete medallion. Join muslin Es to sides of medallion.

2. Referring to *Quilt Top Assembly Diagram*, join 1 dark print A, 44 muslin Bs, 19 light print Bs, 12 dark print Bs, and 4 red print Bs to make 1 outer corner as shown. Repeat to make 4 outer corners. Join 1 muslin D to each outer corner. Join 2 corner units with 1 F as shown to make top unit; repeat to make bottom unit. Join to top and bottom of quilt.

3. To make top pieced border, join 24 muslin Bs and 24 dark print Bs as shown in *Quilt Top Assembly Diagram*. Repeat to make bottom border. Join to top and bottom of quilt. To make 1 side pieced border, join 34 muslin Bs and 34 dark print Bs in same manner; repeat to make second side border. Join to sides of quilt, butting corners.

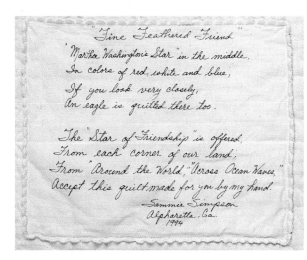

A handwritten documentation block stitched to the back commemorates the special gift and explains the symbolism Sammie used in the design. The top of the block is left open to provide a pocket for a photograph of the quilt and its maker. "That way, the person who receives it will be able to put a face with the quilt," Sammie says. "I hope that, in turn, I can get a picture of the person who receives it."

Quilting

Quilt in-the-ditch around Bs in pieced areas and borders. In large space surrounding central medallion, quilt 4 feather plumes and diagonal lines as shown in photograph.

Finished Edges

Bind with bias binding made from navy.

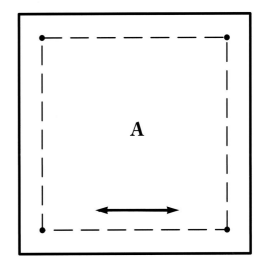

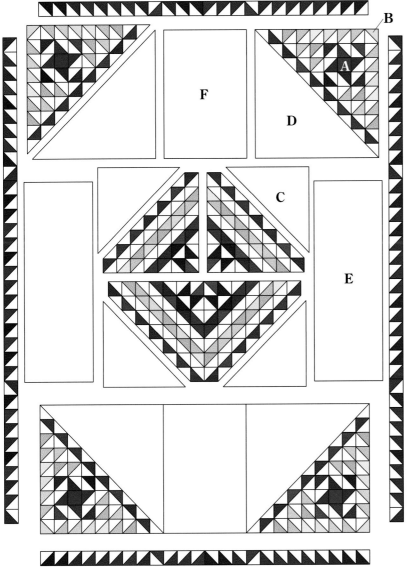

Quilt Top Assembly Diagram

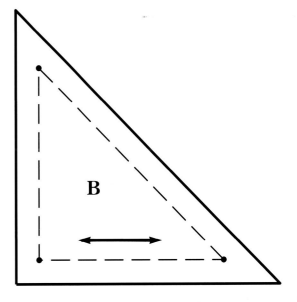

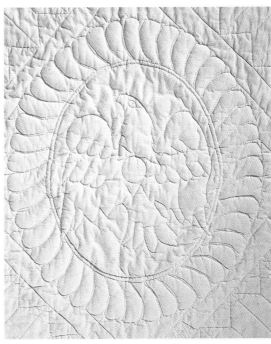

Visible only on the quilt's back, an American eagle is quilted into the central medallion to represent the host country for the 1996 Summer Olympics.

½ Feather Plume Quilting Pattern

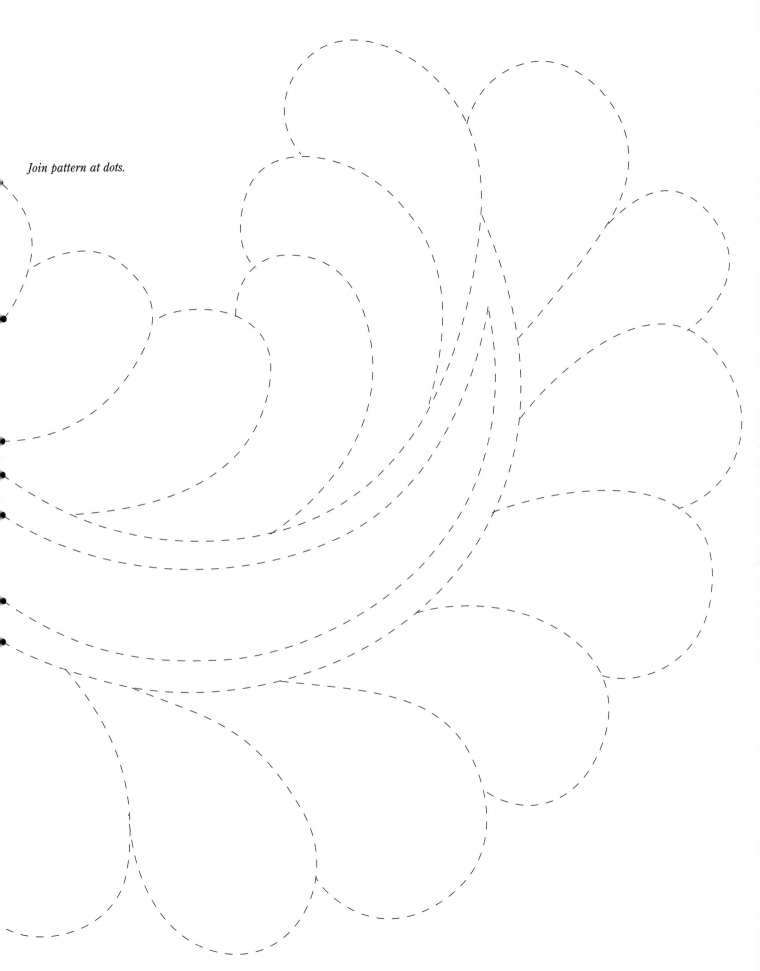

Join pattern at dots.

35

QUILTS ACROSS AMERICA

Freddy Moran
LAFAYETTE, CALIFORNIA

"**I** have an art degree and have worked in the art field all my life," says Freddy Moran. "I consider myself fortunate to have found an area of the arts that is so satisfying."

Although she has been making quilts for only a few years, Freddy has put her art background to good use. "I sit down with graph paper and let my imagination take me where it wants to go," she says of her original designs. She gives away many of her quilts to family and friends and has sold enough pieces to consider herself a professional. Although she works part-time in a local quilt shop, she and her husband still find time to travel, one of their most treasured activities. "We manage to get around the country," she says with a smile. "He plays golf and I go to quilt shops and antiques stores."

Funky Chicken
1994

Freddy designed the Funky Chicken block in a 1994 quilt class called "Natural Forms" taught by Ruth McDowell of Winchester, Massachusetts. According to the class prospectus, each student would be assisted in developing an original design based on a natural theme. "I have no idea how I arrived at this design," says Freddy, "but I love the whimsy of it."

Her classmates also loved the silly little chicken. "For months after I returned home," Freddy says, "my quilting companions sent me chicken fabrics from all over the country. One friend even sent a stuffed chicken. I was a bit fearful of opening packages after that—afraid of receiving a *live* example!"

Several months after that first class, Ruth returned to teach a class based on her book *Symmetry*. "The minute I laid eyes on Ruth's Painted Daisies pattern, I knew my chickens had a place to rest," Freddy says. "I usually sell or give away my quilts, but this one I am going to keep."

Funky Chicken

Finished Quilt Size
77" x 83"

Number of Blocks and Finished Size
40 Chicken blocks	5" x 8"
64 Daisy units	6" x 8"

Fabric Requirements
White	2½ yards
Red stripe	2¼ yards
Brown print	½ yard
Orange	¼ yard
Gold	¼ yard
Red	⅜ yard
Plaids	4 yards
Assorted off-white prints	3¾ yards
Prints for bodies of chickens	1 yard
Prints for background of chicken blocks	1¼ yards
Backing	5½ yards
Binding	1 yard

Pieces to Cut
White
  2 (4" x 77½") border strips
  2 (4" x 76½") border strips
Red stripe
  2 (1½" x 74½") outer borders
  2 (1½" x 70½") outer borders
  2 (1½" x 68½") inner borders
  2 (1½" x 56½") inner borders
  4 (1½" x 8½") strips
Brown print
  64 J
  25 L
Orange
  40 P
Gold
  80 N
Red
  200 N
Plaids*
  64 B
  64 E
  64 H
Assorted off-white prints
  64 A
  64 C
  64 D
  64 F
  64 G
  64 I
  16 K

Prints for bodies of chickens**
  40 M
  40 L
Prints for chicken blocks**
  320 N
  80 O
  40 P
  120 Q
  4 (1½" x 8½") strips

*For each daisy, cut 4 B, 4 E, and 4 H from each plaid.
**For each chicken block, cut 1 M and 1 L of same print for body. Cut 8 N, 2 O, 1 P, and 3 Q from second print for background.

Quilt Top Assembly
1. Referring to *Daisy Unit Assembly Diagram,* join 1 A, 1 B, 1 C, 1 D, 1 E, 1 F, 1 G, 1 H, 1 I, and 1 J in alphabetical order as shown to complete 1 Daisy unit. Repeat, using same colors, to make 4 identical Daisy units. In same manner, repeat to make 64 Daisy units (16 sets of 4).

2. Arrange Daisy units in rows as shown in *Quilt Top Assembly Diagram,* aligning colors and rotating Daisy units as indicated to form daisies.

To complete top row, join Daisy units, 5 Ks, and 5 Ls as shown in *Quilt Top Assembly Diagram.*

To complete second row, join 2 Daisy units, 1 K, and 1 brown print L to make 1 end unit as shown. Referring to *Daisy Block Assembly Diagram,* join next 4 Daisy units with 1 brown L to make 1 Daisy block. Repeat to make 3 Daisy blocks. Join last 2 Daisy units, 1 K, and 1 L to make 1 end unit as shown. Join blocks and end units to complete row.

In same manner, join remaining Daisy units, Ks, and brown Ls into rows. Join rows.

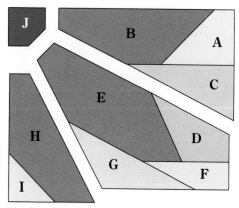

Daisy Unit Assembly Diagram—Make 64.

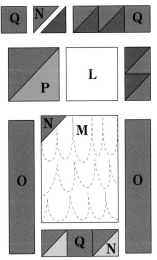

Daisy Block Assembly Diagram

Freddy used many of the chicken fabrics sent by her cross-country quilting friends to piece a colorful, country backing for Funky Chicken.

3. Referring to *Chicken Block Assembly Diagram,* join 1 L, 1 M, 14 Ns, 2 Os, 2 Ps, and 3 Qs as shown to complete 1 Chicken block. Repeat to make 40 Chicken blocks.

Chicken Block Assembly Diagram—Make 40.

4. To make 1 side border, join 7 Chicken blocks in vertical row as shown in *Quilt Top Assembly Diagram.* To 1 long edge of row, join 1½" x 56½" red stripe border. Join to side of quilt with red stripe between quilt top and Chicken blocks. Repeat to make and join second side border.

For top border, make center block by joining 1 (1" x 8½") strip cut from background fabric to 1 long side of 1 Chicken block. Join 5 Chicken blocks to right of center block and 5 to left of center to make horizontal row. Join 1 (1½" x 8½") red stripe piece to each end of row. Join 1 additional Chicken block to each red stripe piece to complete border. Join 1 (1½" x 68½")

red stripe border to bottom edge of pieced Chicken border. Join to top of quilt, butting corners. Repeat to make and join bottom border.

5. Join 1½" x 74½" red stripe borders to sides of quilt. Join 1½" x 70½" red stripe borders to top and bottom of quilt, butting corners.

6. Join 4" x 76½" white borders to sides of quilt. Join 4" x 77½" white borders to top and bottom of quilt, butting corners.

Quilting

Quilt chicken blocks in-the-ditch or as desired. Quilt feathers on chicken bodies as shown on pattern piece M. Quilt body of quilt as desired.

Finished Edges

Bind with bias binding.

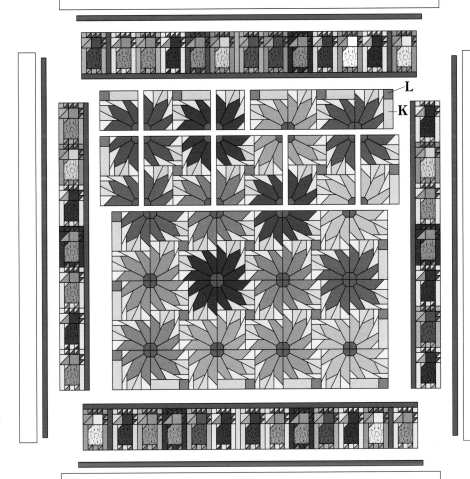

Quilt Top Assembly Diagram

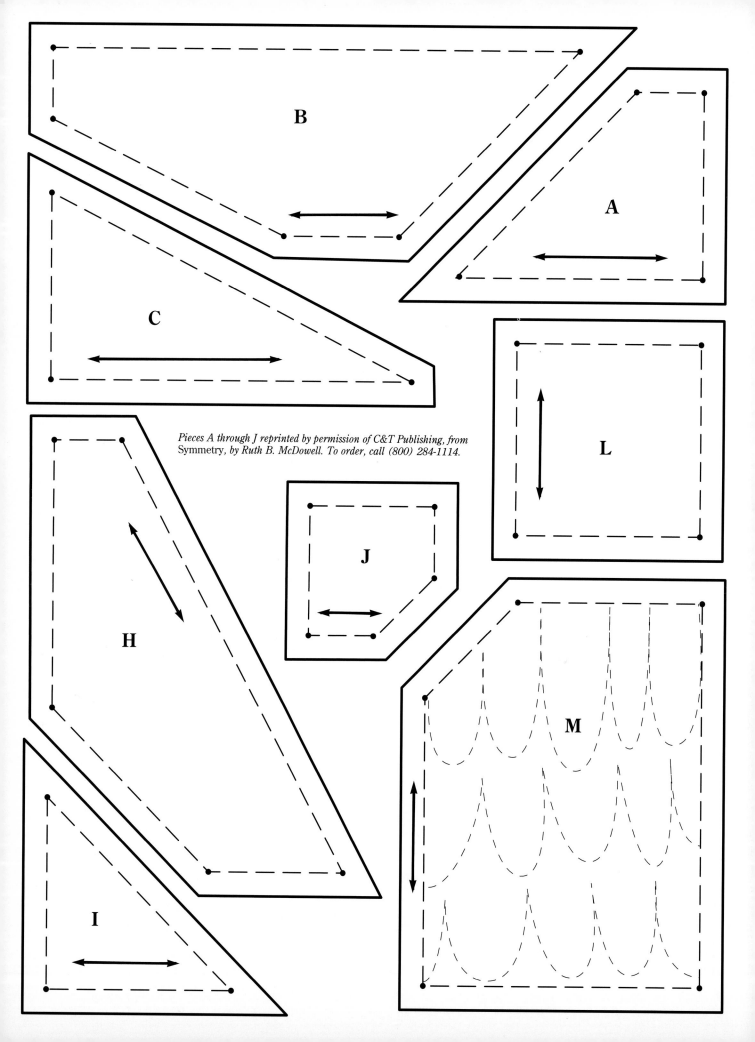

B

A

C

L

Pieces A through J reprinted by permission of C&T Publishing, from Symmetry, *by Ruth B. McDowell. To order, call (800) 284-1114.*

J

H

M

I

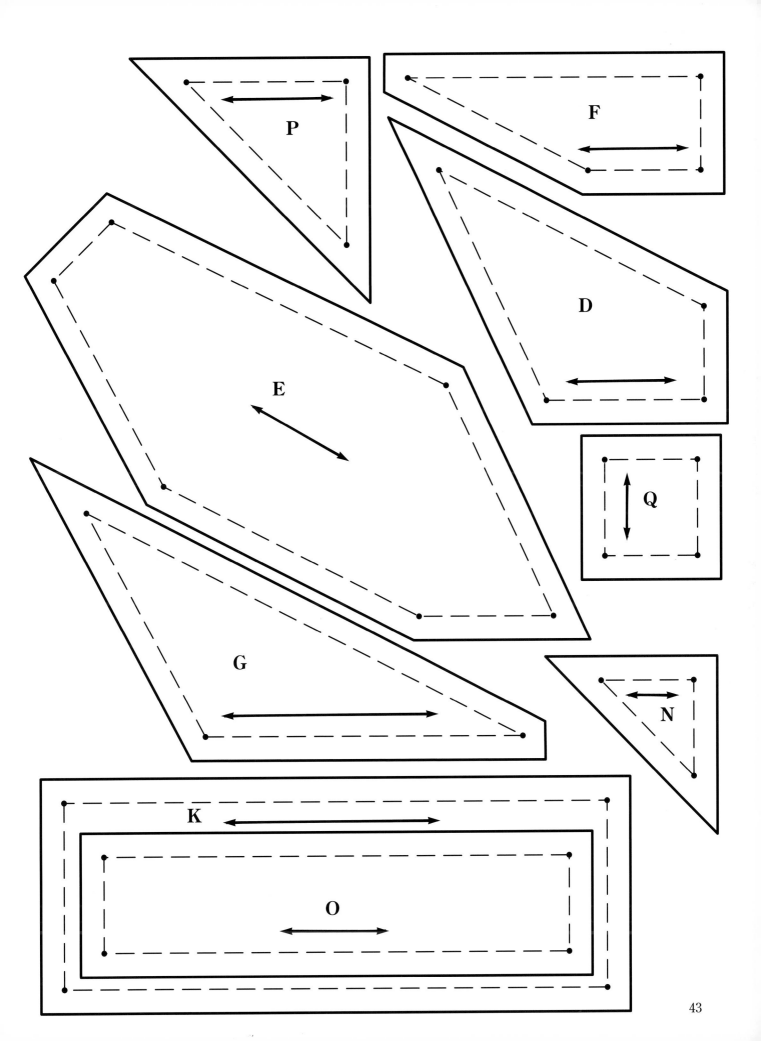

P

F

D

E

Q

G

N

K

O

Sue Nickels
ANN ARBOR, MICHIGAN

A love for needlework runs in Sue Nickels's family. Taught to sew at an early age by their mother, Sue and her sister, Pat, spent many hours sewing and knitting clothes for their dolls. "My mother is an excellent seamstress," Sue says. "I remember the special Halloween costumes she made for us. They are treasured by our family and some have already been enjoyed by the next generation of children."

Sue's love of quilting came from her grandmother, who made simple quilts from scraps and worn clothing. An art degree gave Sue the color and design confidence that shows so well in her work. And the birth of her first child gave her the motivation she needed to begin making quilts.

Sue teaches most aspects of quiltmaking, but her special love is teaching machine quilting. With her sister, she has published a book with Dover Books entitled *60 Quilting Patterns,* and is currently working on another about pieced and appliquéd quilts.

Hark, the Herald Angels Sing
1992

Sue Nickels made *Hark, the Herald Angels Sing* as a gift for her good friend, Sue Holdawey-Heys, who is also a quilter. "The quilt group we belong to has a Christmas exchange," Sue says, "and this was my gift to her. She has a collection of angels, and I thought this would fit nicely in her house at Christmas."

Sue used patterns from one of her favorite books, *Snowbound,* by Red Wagon (see "Resources") and experimented with the setting until she found an arrangement that pleased her. She constructed the quilt entirely by machine, including the flawless appliqué and quilting. "I did this quilt kind of backwards

from the way I usually work," she says. "I usually plan everything ahead of time. But this time I made the different blocks and just laid them out and arranged all the borders and sashing so it would all fit."

Hark, the Herald Angels Sing

Finished Quilt Size
40" x 40"

Fabric Requirements
Blue solid	1¼ yards
Blue print	¾ yard
Pink	1 yard*
Tan	¼ yard
Brown	⅛ yard
Light pink	⅛ yard
Muslin	⅛ yard
Gold	⅛ yard
Red	⅛ yard
Dark red	⅛ yard
Green	⅛ yard
Dark green	⅛ yard

*Includes fabric for bias binding.

Pieces to Cut
Blue solid
  3 (2" x 36½") border strips
  3 A
  3 A rev.
  3 C
  3 C rev.
  3 D
  3 D rev.
  3 (5½" x 7½") F

Blue print
  1 (6½" x 21½") rectangle
  1 (1" x 22") strip
  3 R
  3 R rev.
  3 T
  3 T rev.
  3 V
  3 V rev.
  3 X
  3 X rev.

Pink
  1 (8½" x 26½") rectangle
  3 E
  1 I
  1 I rev.
  4 N

Tan
  3 Q
  3 Q rev.
  3 S
  3 S rev.
  3 U
  3 U rev.
  3 W
  3 W rev.
  3 Y
  3 Y rev.
  6 Z
  6 Z rev.

Brown
  1 (1" x 22") strip
  4 O

Light pink
  3 B
  3 B rev.
Muslin
  3 G
  1 K
  1 K rev.
Gold
  6 (1") squares
  3 H
  2 L
Red
  1 J
  1 J rev.
  1 M
  1 M rev.
  1 (1" x 22") strip
Dark red
  1 (3½" x 21½") rectangle
  1 (1" x 22") strip
Green
  4 P
  1 (1½" x 26½") strip
  1 (1" x 22") strip
Dark green
  1 (1" x 22") strip

Quilt Top Assembly
1. To make star panel, appliqué 4 pink stars (N) to 3½" x 21½" dark red strip, as shown in *Quilt Top Assembly Diagram*. From scraps left after cutting pieces, cut 14 (2" x 1¾") assorted rectangles. Join rectangles along short sides to form pieced strip. Join strip to bottom of star panel, trimming ends of pieced strip even with ends of star panel.

2. To make trumpet angel panel, fold 6½" x 21½" blue rectangle in half vertically to find center line. On right half of rectangle, appliqué 1 I, 1 J, 1 K, 1 L, and 1 M as shown in *Trumpet Angel Appliqué Placement Diagram*. On left half of rectangle, appliqué 1 I rev., 1 J rev., 1 K rev., 1 L, and 1 M rev. as shown. From scraps, cut 14 (2") assorted squares. Join squares to form pieced strip; join strip to bottom of trumpet angel panel. Join top of trumpet angel panel to bottom of star panel/pieced strip completed in Step 1.

3. To make 1 Halo Angel Block, join 1 A, 1 A rev., 1 B, 1 B rev., 1 C, 1 C rev., 1 D, 1 D rev., and 1 E to form body of angel, as shown in *Halo Angel Block Assembly Diagram*. Appliqué 1 G and 1 H to 1 F, taking care to align position of G (head of angel) with E (body of angel) as shown in *Halo Angel Block Assembly Diagram*. Join F

Quilt Top Assembly

1. Referring to *Block Assembly Diagram*, join 1 blue A, 1 blue B, 1 purple print B, 1 dark mauve C, 1 light mauve D, and 1 purple print E as shown to make 1 unit. Repeat to make 4 units. Join to edges of 1 purple print A as shown to complete 1 block. Repeat to make 35 blocks.

2. Join blocks in 7 rows of 5 blocks each. Join rows.

3. Join 1⅛" x 71" blue border strips to sides of quilt. Join 1⅛" x 52" blue border strips to top and bottom of quilt, butting corners.

4. Join 1¾" x 72" purple print middle borders to sides of quilt. Join 2" x 54½" purple print middle borders to top and bottom of quilt, butting corners.

5. To make 1 side pieced border, join 1 light mauve F, 1 dark mauve G, 29 purple print Gs, 14 dark mauve Hs, and 14 light mauve Is as shown in *Quilt Top Assembly Diagram*. Repeat to make second side pieced border. Join to sides of quilt.

To make top border, join 2 purple print Fs, 1 dark mauve G, 21 purple print Gs, 11 dark mauve Hs, and 11 light mauve Is rev. as shown in *Quilt Top Assembly Diagram*. Repeat to make bottom border. Join to top and bottom of quilt, butting corners as shown in *Pieced Border Assembly Diagram*.

6. Join 6½" x 80" purple print outer borders to sides of quilt. Join 6½" x 72½" purple print outer borders to top and bottom of quilt, butting corners. Trim corners as shown in photograph.

Quilting

Quilt in-the-ditch around all pieces in blocks and pieced borders. Quilt outer borders in ¾" cross-hatch pattern, or quilt as desired.

Finished Edges

Bind with bias binding made from purple print.

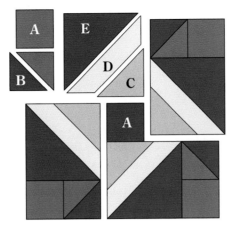

Block Assembly Diagram

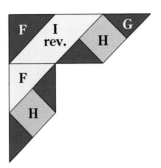

Pieced Border Assembly Diagram

Quilt Top Assembly Diagram

55

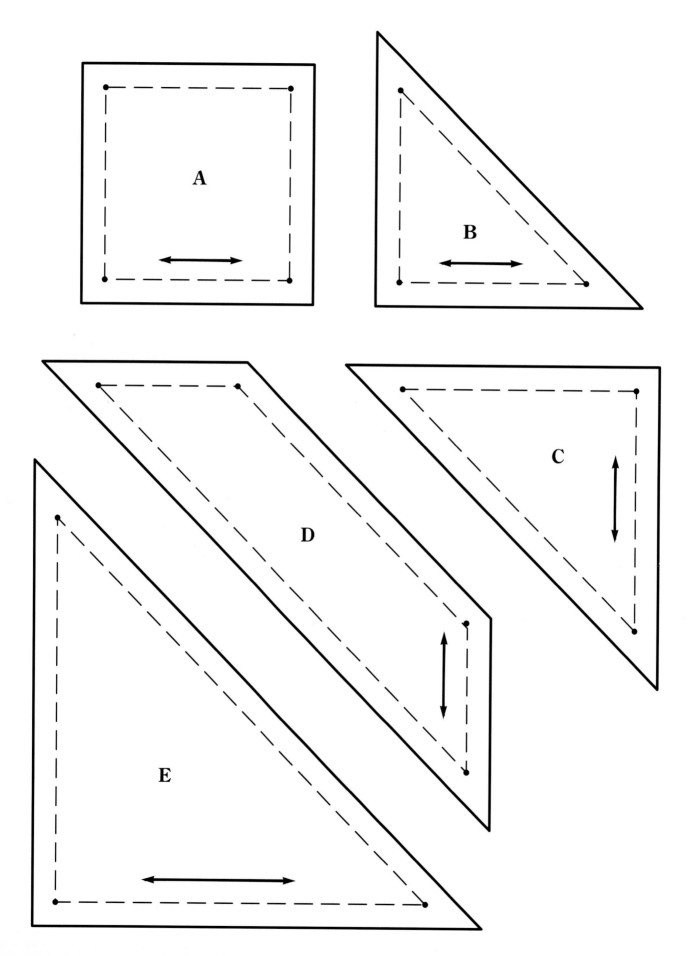

A

B

C

D

E

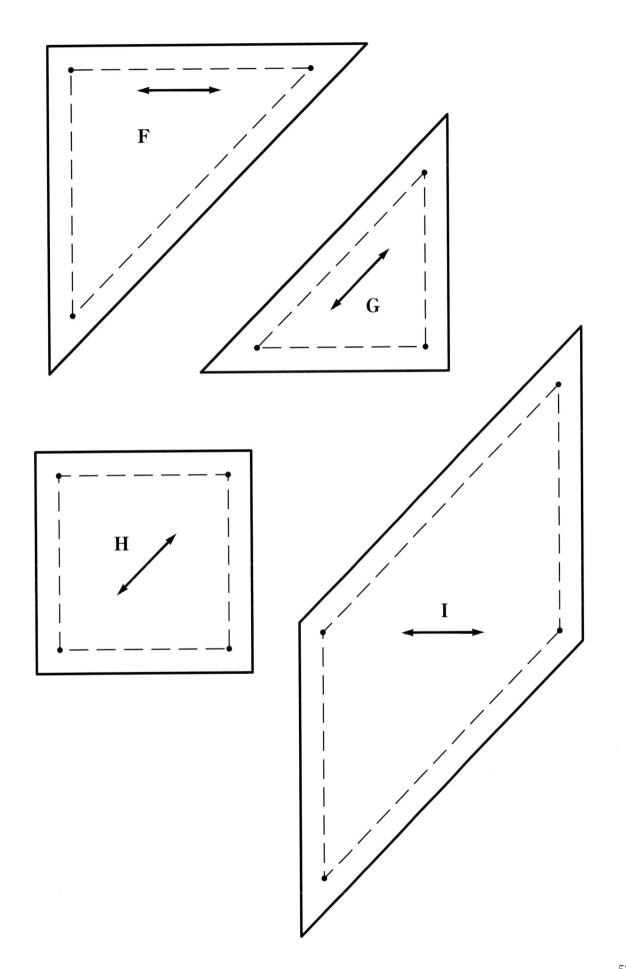

Wendy Hill
NEVADA CITY, CALIFORNIA

Quilt artist Wendy Hill begins the story of her own quiltmaking with the "artist's statement" that accompanied a dinosaur quilt made by a 5-year-old boy. He said, "I did what I did because I wanted to. And my mom helped me with the hard part."

Wendy began sewing at the age of 6 by begging her mother to teach her to make clothes for her dolls. "Two years later, I had this great idea for making a bathrobe by connecting irregular patches of fabric on a base," she says. "My mother couldn't understand what I envisioned, but I now know I wanted to do a crazy-quilted bathrobe!" The crazy bathrobe never came into being, but Wendy sewed clothing "from tailored to wacko" for herself through high school. In 1971 she began making traditional quilts, teaching herself from the few books available. Combining the techniques of quiltmaking with the art she had studied in college, Wendy began developing original designs in 1986. Most of her original quilts since then have been designed as wall hangings, with a few exceptions.

"When my son was 3," Wendy says, "I told him I was going to make a quilt just for him. He was so pleased and excited, and wanted to know right away which wall it was going on. He had never known about quilts being used as blankets!"

At Cross Purposes Again
1992

At Cross Purposes Again is Wendy's second quilt made from her original "almost triangle" block. "I intended to draft a block for a basic bed quilt," Wendy says. "I collected 27 fabrics for it, none of which my husband liked. So I made the size smaller and made a quilt for the wall with those 27 dreaded fabrics. Of course, it's his

favorite! I called that quilt *Cross Purposes.*" Playing further with the block, Wendy began brainstorming ideas, jotting notes and sketches, and making small-scale glued mockups. She found that string-piecing each "almost triangle" on a foundation gave her the under-and-over color effect she was seeking; working

with opposite pairs of colors made the blocks seem to weave around the sashing strips.

"This block is a chameleon," Wendy says. "With or without sashing, it can look like pinwheels, braided designs, nine patch, or a random contemporary design."

We've slightly simplified Wendy's construction technique to increase the ease of piecing the "almost triangle" blocks. Notice also that Wendy deliberately cut the gray striped sashing strips so that the stripes would not line up at the intersections. "This increases the tension in the design," she says.

At Cross Purposes Again

Finished Quilt Size
53¾" x 53¾"

Number of Blocks and Finished Size
24 blocks   7½" x 7½"

Fabric Requirements*
Gray stripe	1½ yards
White	½ yard
Yellow	¾ yard
Red	¾ yard
Purple	½ yard
Gray	½ yard
Black	¾ yard
Backing	3½ yards
Silver lamé piping	7 yards

Other Materials (Optional)*
Tracing paper	
1 pad (100 sheets)	14" x 17"
OR	
Tear-away stabilizer	
(22" wide)	4¼ yards

Pieces to Cut*
Gray stripe
  24 A
  16 E
  64 H
White
  4 B
  13 C
  6 D
  2 F
  2 G
Yellow
  9 B
  15 C
  7 D
  4 F
  3 G

Red
  2 B
  6 C
  1 D
  1 F
  1 G
Purple
  3 B
  14 C
  2 D
  3 F
  3 G
Gray
  6 B
  8 C
  5 D
  2 F
  2 G
Black
  2 B
  30 C
  5 D
  4 F
  5 G
*See Step 1.

Quilt Top Assembly

1. Pieces B, C, D, F, and G in Wendy Hill's quilt were string-pieced to increase the variety of fabrics and the complexity of the overall design. If you choose to string-piece, you will need several fabrics of each color; use scraps or buy amounts to total the yardages given above *plus* ¼ yard each. From foundation material (tracing paper or tear-away stabilizer), cut 26 Bs, 86 Cs, 26 Ds, 16 Fs, and 16 Gs. Divide foundations into groups for each color. (See Pieces to Cut.) Follow steps in **Quilt Smart** on page 61 to complete string piecing.

2. Following *Block 1 Assembly Diagram* and referring to *Quilt Top Assembly Diagram* for color placement, join 1 A, 1 B, 3 Cs, and 1 D to make 1 Block 1. Repeat to make 22 Block 1s. Following *Block 2 Assembly Diagram* and referring to *Quilt Top Assembly Diagram* for color placement, join 1 A, 2 Bs, 2 Cs, and 2 Ds to make 1 Block 2. Repeat to make 2 Block 2s. Following *Half-Block Assembly Diagram*, join 1 C, 1 E, 1 F, and 1 G to make 1 Half-Block. Repeat to make 16 Half-Blocks.

3. Following *Quilt Top Assembly Diagram*, join blocks, half-blocks, and sashing strips (H) into diagonal rows, rotating Block 1s as indicated by arrows. Join rows.

Quilting

Quilt in-the-ditch around all sashing strips. Quilt blocks and half-blocks with diagonal cross-hatching lines 1¼" apart, leaving outermost ½" of quilt unquilted.

Finished Edges

Fold outside edges of backing away from edge of quilt; pin in place. On front of quilt, align raw edge of piping with raw edge of quilt top; pin in place, taking care to catch top and batting only. Stitch. Fold piping out, smoothing seam allowance of piping, top, and batting toward center of quilt. Unpin backing. Fold seam allowance of backing under, matching fold line to stitched line of piping. Handstitch backing in place. Complete quilting to edges.

Quilt Top Assembly Diagram

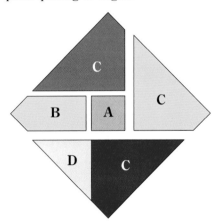

Block 1 Assembly Diagram

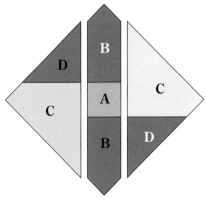

Block 2 Assembly Diagram

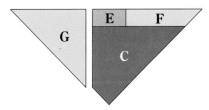

Half-Block Assembly Diagram

❖ Quilt Smart

String Piecing

Place 1 strip of fabric right side up on 1 foundation piece. Strip must be long enough to go across foundation and extend ¼" at each end. Place second strip right side down on top of first strip, aligning 1 long edge. Stitch, using a ¼" seam.

Flip second strip right side up and press; place next strip.

Continue in same manner (*Figure 1*) until foundation piece is covered (*Figure 2*).

Turn completed piece over. Trim excess fabric from edges (*Figure 3*). Remove foundation material. (You may need to slightly dampen tracing paper to completely remove all bits.)

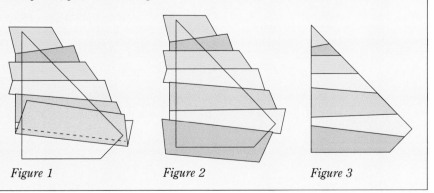

Figure 1   *Figure 2*   *Figure 3*

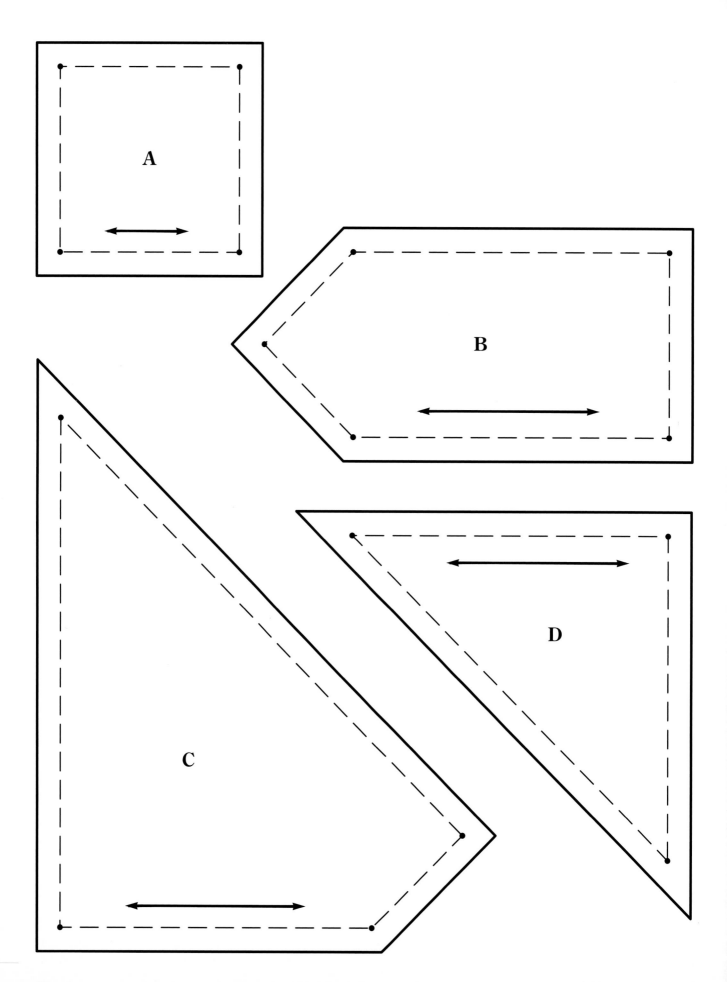

A

B

C

D

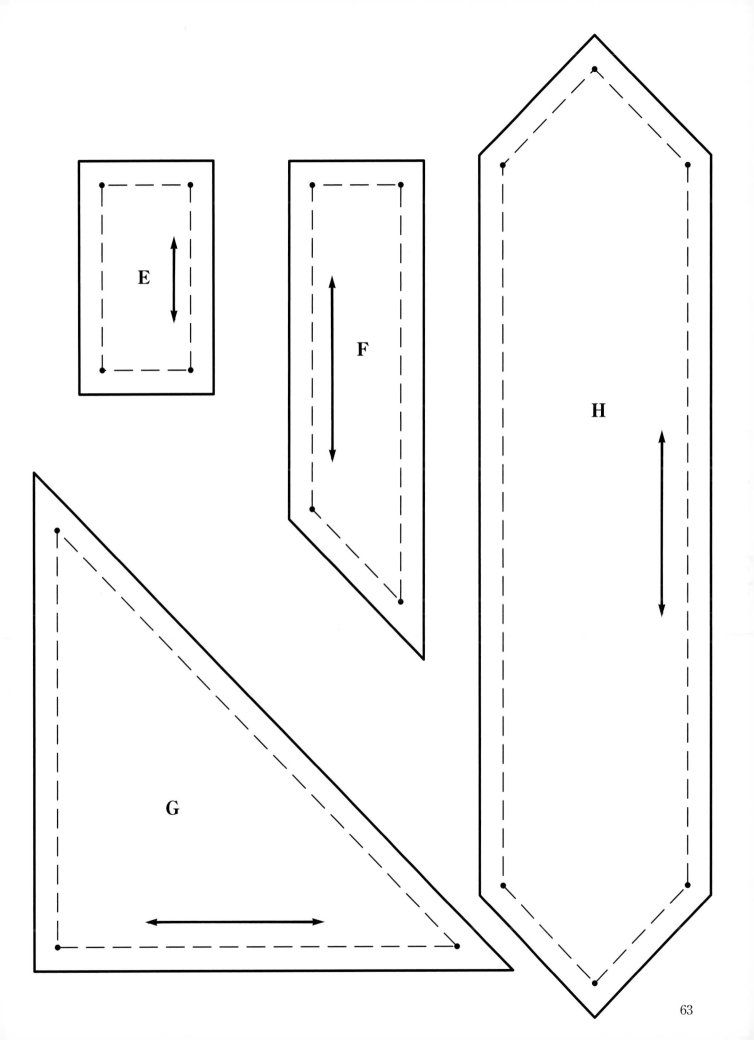

E

F

G

H

63

"The intrinsic combination of function and beauty—that's what I like about quilts."

Virginia Jones
TAUNTON, MASSACHUSETTS

"**M**y story is typical of many quilters," says Virginia Jones. "I dabbled in handcrafts for 30 years, but I never considered myself a creative person until I started quilting."

Although she had been fascinated by quilting for many years, Virginia did not make her first quilt until 1989, when two circumstances coincided. "The rotary cutter had come into common use," she says, "and I needed to make gifts for several special weddings that all happened one summer." Since then, she has completed about 35 quilts and has another dozen tops waiting to be pieced. "I'm strictly self-taught," she says. "I read everything I can on the subject and attend every quilt show within a reasonable distance."

Several years ago, Virginia built a barn-shaped addition to her home, the expansion that would provide the spark for *North Elevation*. "The architect thought that the new wing, built next to the kitchen, would be a dining room. But I knew from the start it was a quilting studio, complete with a skylight and storage for my fabrics."

North Elevation: A Barn for Virginia
1993

"I made this quilt to celebrate the addition to my house," says Virginia. "Like the building, the quilt grew from a small project to a major one!"

Virginia had originally planned her quilt as a medallion-centered wall hanging measuring about 40" x 60". But playing with the colors and values of the blocks entranced her, and *North Elevation* ended up almost twice the size she had planned.

Even so, she completed it in about five months, spurred on by the deadline to enter the Eastcoast Quilters Alliance competition with the theme "A View That's New."

"I used appliqué in this quilt, a technique that is new to me," Virginia says. "The increased sophistication in the use of color also represents a new view. The quilt also represents a literal view that's

new: the addition to my house in the shape of a barn."

Virginia's rush to meet the deadline was well rewarded. *North Elevation* won the Directors' Choice prize in the Eastcoast Quilters Alliance show. And in June of 1994, it also won first place in the pieced category at the West Texas Quilt Show in San Angelo, Texas.

North Elevation: A Barn for Virginia

Finished Quilt Size
68" x 93½"

Number of Blocks and Finished Size

154 Barn Door blocks	6" x 6"
34 Half Barn Door blocks	6" x 6"
1 Barn block	12" x 12"

Pieces to Cut

White
  1 (17") square
  1 (¾" x 15") strip*
Gray print
  1 (12½") square
Black
  1 (1" x 15") strip*
  2 (5⅛") squares**
Gray and black prints***
  684 A
  684 B
  154 C
  68 I
Red prints†
  650 A
  684 B
  68 I

*See Step 1.
**Cut squares in half diagonally for 4 corner triangles.
***For each block, cut 4 As, 4 Bs, and 1 C of same print. For each half-block, cut 2 As, 2 Bs, and 2 Is of same black print.
†For each block, cut 4 As and 4 Bs of same print. For each half-block, cut 1 A, 2 Bs, and 2 Is of same print.

Fabric Requirements

White	½ yard
Black	½ yard
Gray and black prints	5¼ yards
Red prints	4¼ yards
Backing	5¾ yards
Black for bias binding	1 yard

Quilt Top Assembly

1. Join 1" x 15" black strip to ¾" x 15" white strip along long edges. Press seam open. Aligning dashed line on pattern pieces with seam line, cut 1 E, 1 E rev., 1 H, and 1 H rev. from pieced strip.

2. From 17" white square, cut 1 (1" x 24") bias strip. Fold in half lengthwise; press. Referring to *Bias Strip Appliqué Diagram,* appliqué bias strip to D, following placement lines on pattern piece.

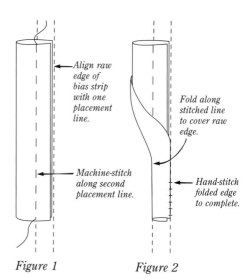

← *Align raw edge of bias strip with one placement line.*

Fold along stitched line to cover raw edge.

← *Machine-stitch along second placement line.*

← *Hand-stitch folded edge to complete.*

Figure 1   *Figure 2*

Bias Strip Appliqué Diagram

3. Referring to *Appliqué Placement Diagram,* appliqué barn (D) to center of 12½" gray square. Arrange G and F to form cupola as shown in diagram; appliqué to gray square. Join E to E rev. along angled ends to form roof; appliqué. Join H to H rev. in same manner; appliqué to top of cupola to complete barn block.

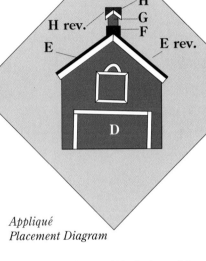

Appliqué
Placement Diagram

4. Referring to *Block Assembly Diagram,* join 4 red print As, 4 gray or black As, 4 red print Bs, 4 gray or black Bs, and 1 gray or black C as shown to complete 1 Hole in the Barn Door block. Repeat to make 154 blocks.

5. Referring to *Half-Block Assembly Diagram,* join 1 red print A, 2 black print As, 2 red print Bs, 2 black print Bs, 2 red print Is, and 2 black print Is as shown to complete 1 half-block. Repeat to make 34 half-blocks.

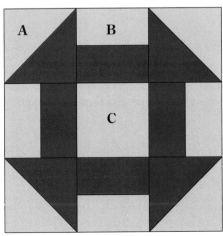

Block Assembly Diagram—Make 154.

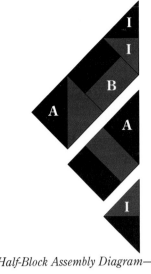

Half-Block Assembly Diagram—Make 34.

6. Referring to *Quilt Top Assembly Diagram,* arrange appliquéd barn block, Hole in the Barn Door blocks, half-blocks, and corner triangles in diagonal rows as shown. Join blocks into rows. Join rows.

Quilting
Quilt in-the-ditch or as desired. Quilt *Weather Vane Quilting Pattern* on top of cupola.

Finished Edges
Bind with bias binding made from black.

Corner triangle

Quilt Top Assembly Diagram

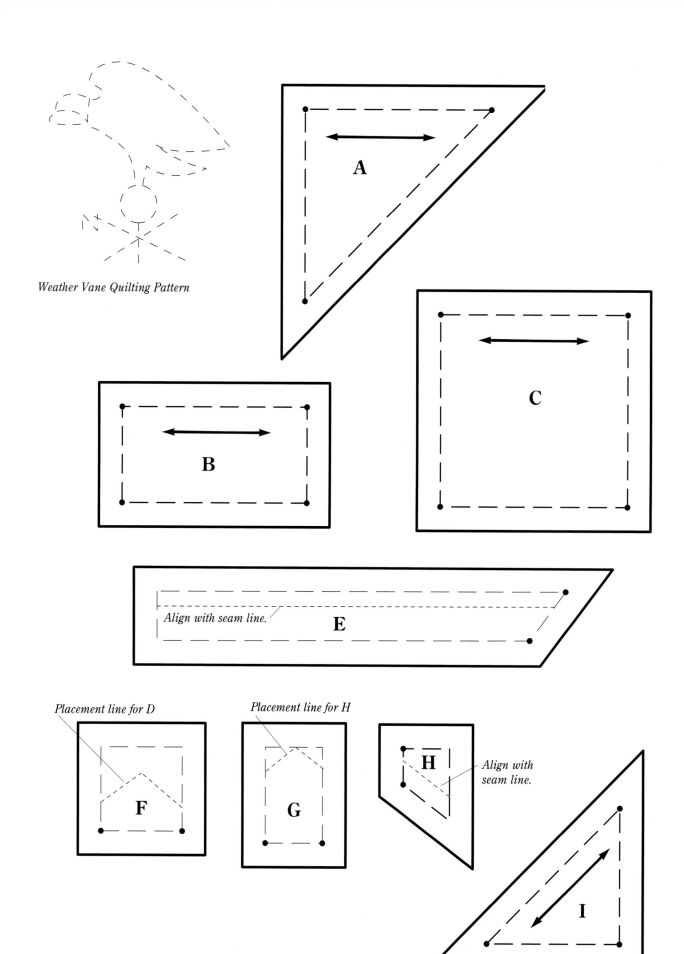

Weather Vane Quilting Pattern

A

B

C

E

Align with seam line.

Placement line for D

F

Placement line for H

G

H

Align with
seam line.

I

68

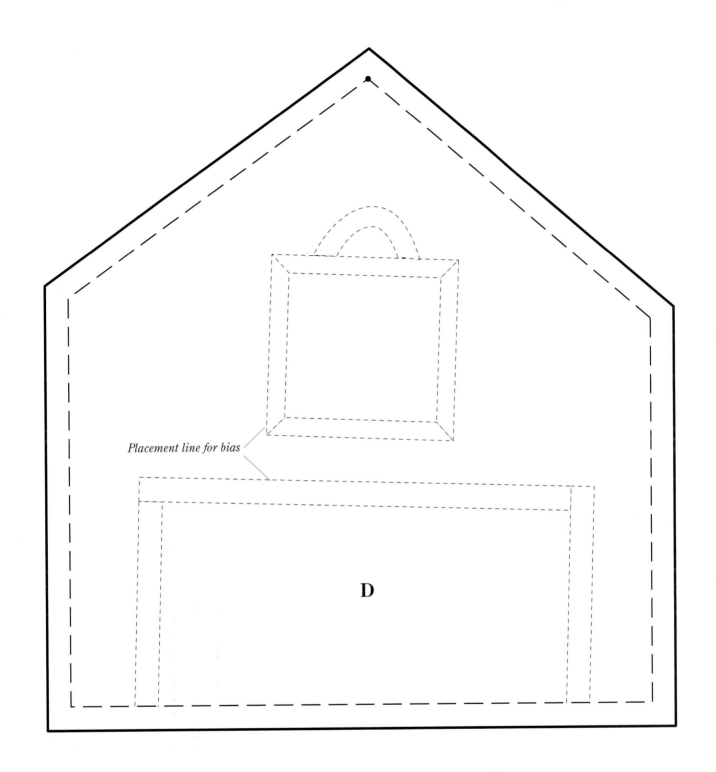

Placement line for bias

D

"I like scrap quilts best. Using many fabrics in a quilt keeps me interested throughout the project."

Maggie Dupuis
DAVISON, MICHIGAN

"The only part of my house that doesn't have some part of the quilting process going on is the bathroom!" says Maggie Dupuis.

Maggie began quilting six years ago after undergoing surgery on her hand. Because she could not do the fine hand sewing she had been doing for years, she turned to quilting and began using rotary-cutting, machine-piecing, and machine-quilting techniques. As a result, she has finished an incredible number of quilts—more than 200—in those six years. How are all those quilts used? "On the boys' beds," she says, "on the walls, to cover or wrap up in (this *is* Michigan, after all), to fill my quilt cupboard, and to overflow to my sister's and Mom's houses!"

A design engineering supervisor, Maggie designs all her quilts on computer. Her ideas come from many sources, including pictures, fabrics, and discussions with other quilters. "I've concentrated my education and professional career in a male-dominated field," Maggie says. "Quilting is the first time in my life I've had the chance to deal with women other than family or work friends, so this has been a new and enjoyable experience for me."

Richard's Kala Mojakka
1991

At the request of her friend Ami Simms, Maggie made this quilt from a design Ami wanted to include in her book *Classic Quilts: Designs from Ancient Rome*. "This one looked like fish to me," Maggie says, "and fish were interesting because I have lived near the Great Lakes most of my life." Maggie and her husband, Richard, lived at that time near Lake Superior on the Upper Peninsula

of Michigan, an area with many Finnish-speaking fishermen. Richard sailed for part of each year with a Finnish crew who taught him many of their phrases, including *kala mojakka* (pronounced *CALL-a MOY-a-kuh*) or "fish stew."

"The quilting patterns are from my life on Lake Michigan," says Maggie. "The ropes and fishing floats would wash up on the beach, and we would

collect them and sell them back to the local commercial fisherman who had lost them off his nets!" Maggie also quilted a fishbone pattern in each of the fishes. The border is pieced in a herringbone pattern. "Rich keeps referring to the border as fish sticks," Maggie says. "There's a lot of fish in this fish stew!"

Richard's Kala Mojakka

Finished Quilt Size
55½" x 69½"

Number of Blocks and Finished Size
12 blocks   14" x 14"

Fabric Requirements
Dark prints   2½ yards
Light prints   3¾ yards
Beige   2¼ yards
Backing   3½ yards
Dark print
    for bias binding   ¾ yard

Pieces to Cut
Dark prints
    48 A
    42 (1⅛" x 25") strips for pieced
         border
Light prints
    48 B*
    48 B rev.*
    43 (1⅛" x 25") strips for pieced
         border
    144 (1⅛" x 4½") strips for C**
Beige
    2 (2¼" x 70") outer border strips
    2 (2¼" x 56½") outer border strips
    2 (2¼" x 60") inner border strips
    2 (2¼" x 46") inner border strips
    12 D
    4 E

*Cut 2 B and 2 B rev. from each print.
**See Step 1.

Quilt Top Assembly

1. To make piece C, join 3 (1⅛" x 4½") light strips along long edges. Referring to *Cutting Diagram for Piece C* (page 75), place pattern made from template C over pieced unit, aligning seam lines. (Note that there will be a gap at the corner where the pieced unit does not fully cover the pattern; this gap will be covered later by piece D.) Cut along solid cutting lines for 1 C. Repeat to make 48 Cs.

2. Referring to *Block Assembly Diagram 1*, join 1 A, 1 B, 1 B rev., and 1 C to make 1 unit as shown. Repeat to make 4 units; join units. Appliqué 1 D over center of Cs to complete 1 block, as shown in *Block Assembly Diagram 2*. Repeat to make 12 blocks.

3. Referring to *Quilt Top Assembly Diagram* and photograph for color placement, join blocks into 4 rows of 3 blocks each, placing same light prints adjacent to each other where possible. Join rows.

4. Join 2¼" x 46" beige inner borders to top and bottom of quilt. Join 2¼" x 60" beige inner borders to sides of quilt, mitering corners.

5. To make pieced borders, join 1⅛" x 25" print strips along long edges, alternating light and dark. Cutting at 45° angle to seam lines, cut 8 (34"-long) strips for side borders and 8 (27"-long) strips for top and bottom borders.

Referring to *Border Piecing Diagram*, join 1 E and 4 (34"-long) pieced strips as shown, alternating dark and light colors in top and bottom strips, to make 1 side border. Repeat to make second side border. In same manner, join remaining Es and pieced strips to make top and bottom borders. Join borders to quilt, mitering corners.

6. Join 2¼" x 56½" beige outer borders to top and bottom of quilt. Join 2¼" x 70" beige borders to sides of quilt, mitering corners.

Quilting

Quilt in-the-ditch around As and Cs. Quilt circles in center of each block. Quilt random stipple pattern across remainder of background. Quilt *Fishbone Quilting Pattern* in each A. Quilt *Rope Quilting Pattern* in beige borders. Quilt *Fishing Float Quilting Pattern* in pieced border.

Finished Edges

Bind with bias binding made from dark print.

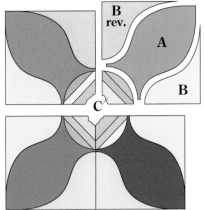
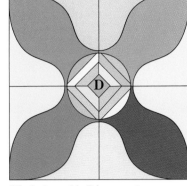

Block Assembly Diagram 1   *Block Assembly Diagram 2*

Quilt Top Assembly Diagram

Border Piecing Diagram

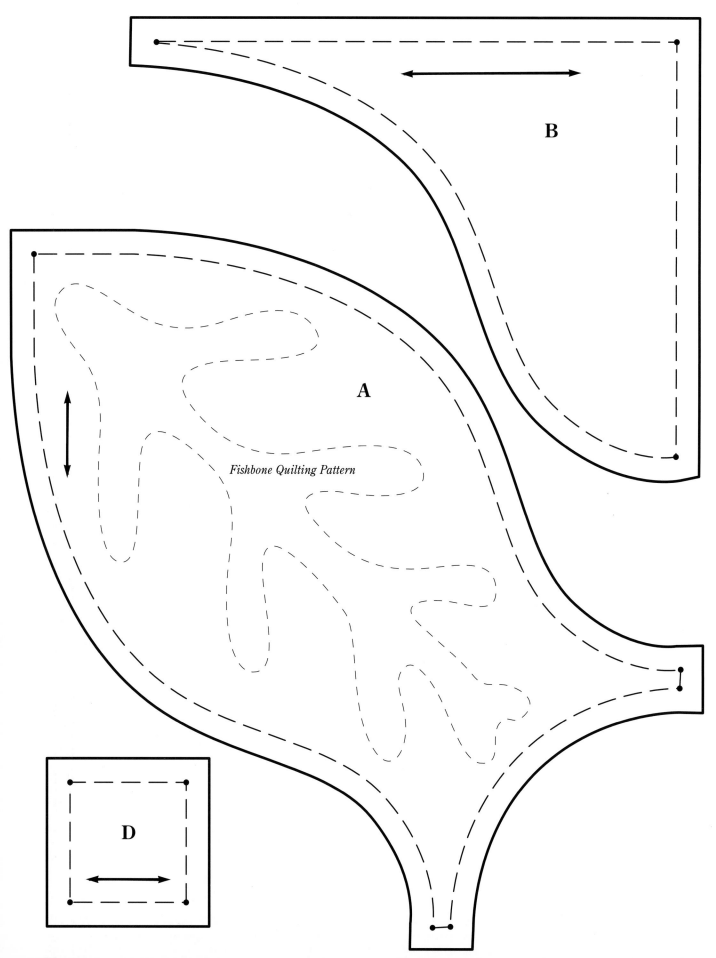

B

A

Fishbone Quilting Pattern

D

74

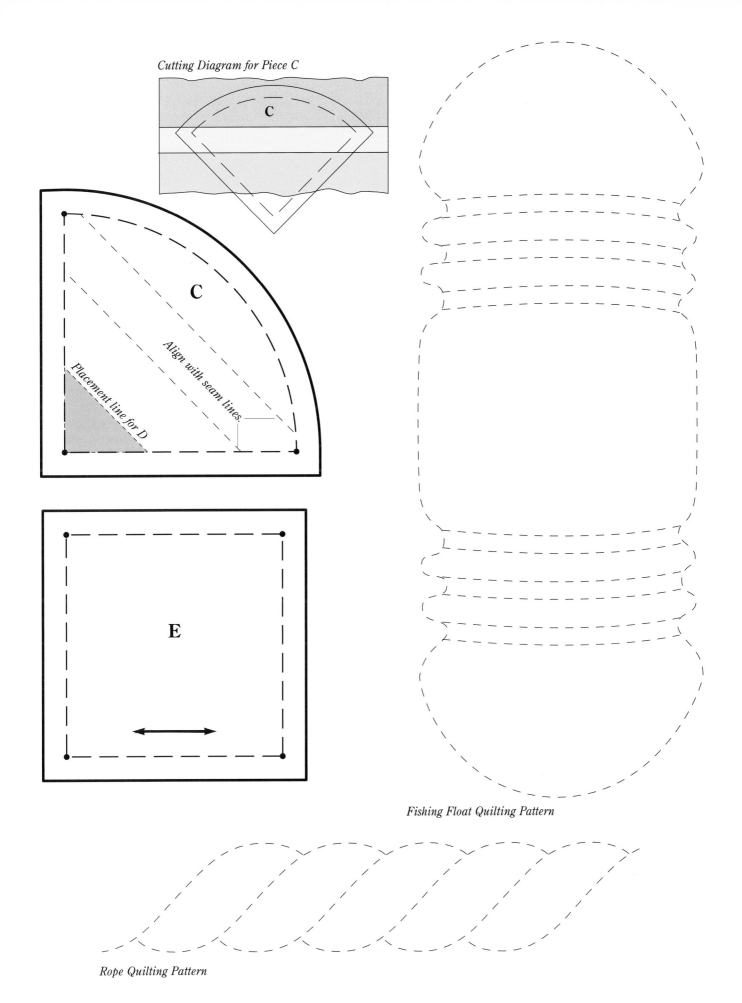

Cutting Diagram for Piece C

C

C

Align with seam lines.

Placement line for D

E

Fishing Float Quilting Pattern

Rope Quilting Pattern

75

TRADITIONS IN QUILTING

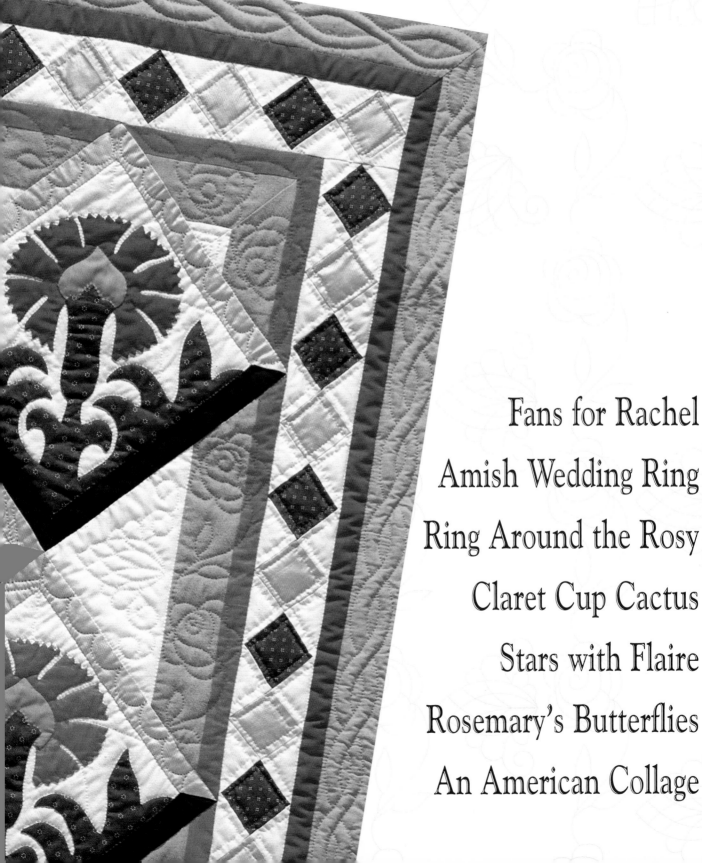

"My quilts will be around after I am gone, and that means that the love I put into them will live on, too."

Nancy Oberst Clark
CHESHIRE, CONNECTICUT

Nancy Oberst Clark can't remember a time when she wasn't creating with her hands. "I was blessed with parents who believed in spending free time creatively," says Nancy. Her love for quilting bloomed shortly after her hometown's bicentennial in 1980, when she decided to teach herself to quilt.

Now a full-time quilter, Nancy is the quilting instructor for the local Adult Education program. She offers workshops on many techniques, including *broderie perse,* sashiko, crazy quilting, and string quilting. Although she does sell some of her smaller quilts, Nancy regards her quilting primarily as an expression of love for her family. Each year she donates a quilt to the adoption agency that located her Korean daughter, Rachel. "I feel that I am leaving something of myself to future generations," says Nancy. "My quilts will be around after I am gone, and that means that the love I put into them will live on, too."

Shown here with her special quilt is Nancy's daughter, Rachel So Hee Clark, at age 3.

Fans for Rachel
1991

Fans for Rachel is a quilt of pure celebration, made while Nancy and her husband were waiting for the arrival of their adopted daughter from South Korea. "I wanted to create a unique quilt for her that would have an Asian flair," Nancy says, "while incorporating the traditions of sashiko quilting." Each of the sashiko patterns in the quilt bear special meaning for Nancy's family. (See page 82 and Quilt Smart on page 83.) "Rachel is very possessive of this quilt, knowing it was made especially for her," says Nancy. "When I look at it, I recall the intense excitement I felt while waiting for our beautiful little daughter to join our family."

Quilt Top Assembly

1. Referring to *Block Assembly Diagram,* join 9 blue print As to form fan. Turn under ¼" along top edge of each A; press or baste in place.

On 1 white 12½" square, lightly mark a point 1¼" from 1 corner along 1 side; mark a second point 1¼" from opposite corner along adjacent side. Place fan on white square, aligning tops of outer As with marked points. Appliqué top edges of As to square.

Turn under ¼" along top edge of heart (B), clipping seam allowance at point and at side dots. Press or baste in place. Aligning lower edge of B with raw edge of square, appliqué top edge of B to fan to complete 1 block. If desired, turn square over and cut away excess white fabric under appliqué. Repeat to make 8 blocks.

2. Referring to *Quilt Top Assembly Diagram,* join blocks, side triangles, and corner triangles in diagonal rows as shown. Join rows.

3. Join 4½" x 51½" blue solid border strips to sides of quilt. To make top border, join 1 (4½") yukata square to each end of 1 (4½" x 34½") blue solid border strip. Repeat to make bottom border. Join to top and bottom of quilt, butting corners.

Quilting

Outline-quilt edges of As, Bs, and scalloped top of fan. In white portion of fan blocks, quilt *Seigaiha (Ocean Waves) Quilting Pattern.* In side triangles, quilt *Lotus Quilting Pattern.* In corner triangles, quilt central 3 lobes of *Lotus Quilting Pattern.* In borders, quilt *Shippou (Seven Treasures) Quilting Pattern.*

Finished Edges

Bind with bias binding made from blue solid.

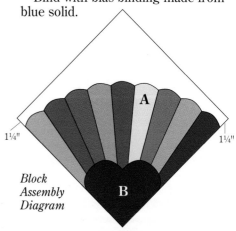

Block Assembly Diagram

Fans for Rachel

Finished Quilt Size
42" x 59"

Number of Blocks and Finished Size
8 blocks   12" x 12"

Fabric Requirements
White	2 yards
Blue solid	2¼ yards*
Blue prints	2¼ yards**
Yukata	½ yard***
Backing	2 yards

*Includes fabric for bias binding.
**Buy ¼ yard each of 9 prints.
***See "Resources."

Pieces to Cut
White
  8 (12½") squares
  2 (18¼") squares†
  2 (9⅜") squares††
Blue solid
  2 (4½" x 51½") border strips
  2 (4½" x 34½") border strips
Blue prints
  72 A
Yukata
  4 (4½") squares
  8 B

†Cut into quarters diagonally for 6 side
  triangles. (You will have 2 left over.)
††Cut in half diagonally for 4 corner
  triangles.

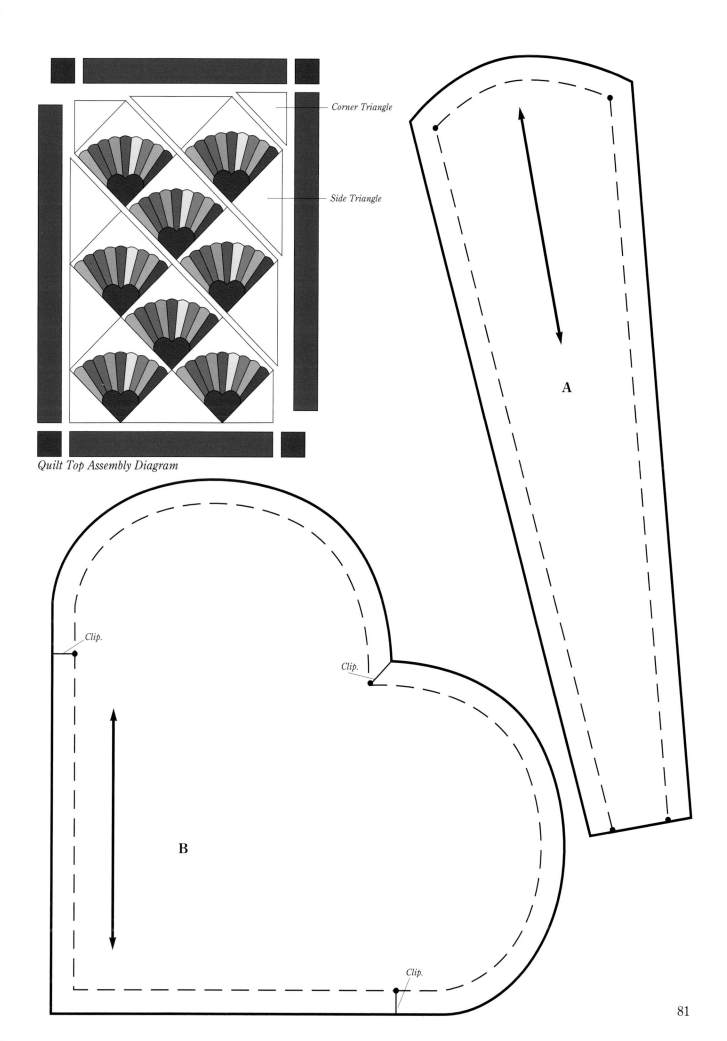

Quilt Top Assembly Diagram

Corner Triangle

Side Triangle

A

B

Clip.

Clip.

Clip.

81

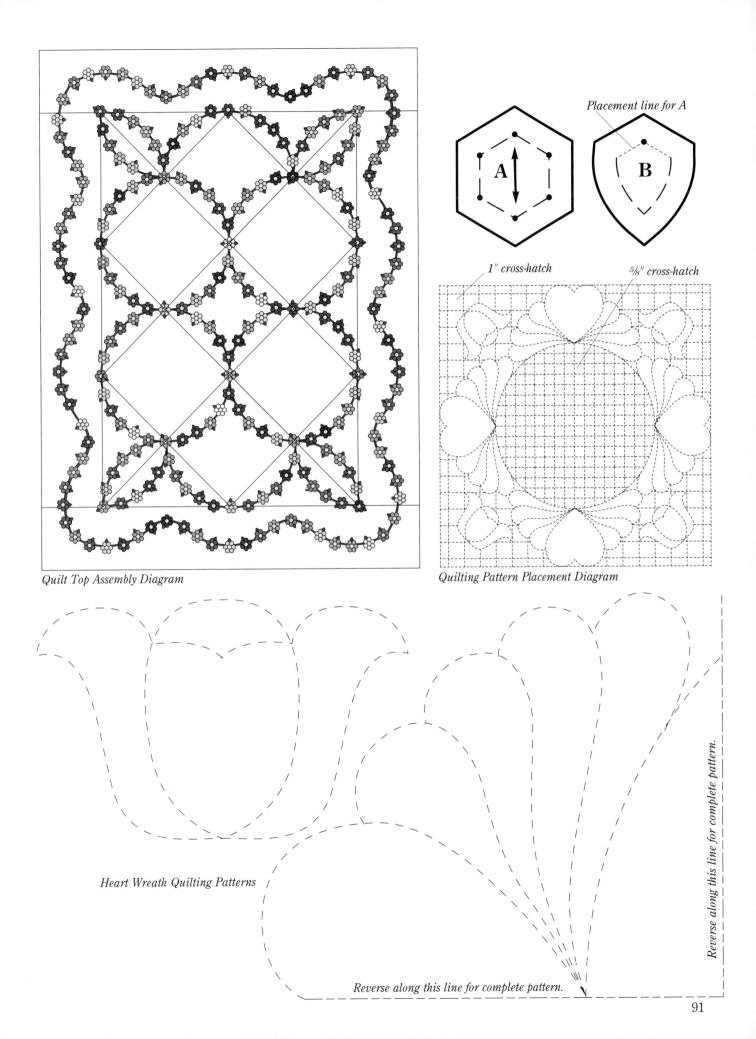

Quilt Top Assembly Diagram

Placement line for A

A

B

1" cross-hatch   ⅝" cross-hatch

Quilting Pattern Placement Diagram

Heart Wreath Quilting Patterns

Reverse along this line for complete pattern.

Reverse along this line for complete pattern.

91

Laverne Noble Mathews
ORANGE, TEXAS

"Although I didn't realize it until later in life, I do have a quilting heritage," says Laverne Mathews. "My mother made quilts for us children, I helped quilt on church quilts as a child, and somewhere along the line I inherited a Double Wedding Ring, but they were not memorable at the time. It wasn't until 1971 that the desire to make a Lone Star quilt swept over me, full-blown."

That itch has led Laverne, like many who fell in love with the craft at that time, to a life-long involvement with fabric, color, and design. "I love to read museum catalogs and state documentation books to get the ideas flowing," she says. "The complicated quilts of the early to middle nineteenth century, with those wonderful old fabrics, are my favorites." Most of her ideas, like *Claret Cup Cactus,* are original. "I find pleasure in each of the steps in quiltmaking," Laverne says, "but planning and executing that first block give me the most satisfaction."

Claret Cup Cactus
1987

"Claret Cups are gorgeous cactus blooms with wonderful color, seen in the Big Bend area of west Texas," explains Laverne. "The *Texas Highways* magazine can't resist publishing pictures of them each year."

When she decided to make a quilt celebrating the Claret Cup cactus, Laverne developed her design using a technique she has taught in workshops for her guild and for school children. "A square of paper was folded only once on the diagonal," she explains, "and then cut freehand to make leaves on two edges with the flower shape in the middle."

Claret Cup Cactus has won a number of awards, including first place ribbons at the 1987 Gulf States Quilting Association show and the 1989 Dallas Quilt Celebration. And in November of 1993, it was published in *McCall's Quilting.*

Claret Cup Cactus

Finished Quilt Size
42" x 59"

Number of Blocks and Finished Size
18 blocks   12" x 12"

Fabric Requirements
Tan	2½ yards
Gold	2 yards
Assorted reds	1¾ yards
Green	1¼ yards
Dark green	½ yard
Blue	½ yard
Backing	4 yards
Green for bias binding	¾ yard

Pieces to Cut
Tan
   5 (5" x 32") strips
   4 (1½" x 32") strips
   18 (8½") squares
   160 F
   16 G

Gold
   2 (2¼" x 64") outer border strips
   2 (2¼" x 51") outer border strips
   9 (2⅜" x 32") strips
   18 B

Assorted reds
   2 (1⅜" x 60½") inner border strips
   2 (1⅜" x 47") inner border strips
   9 (1⅜" x 32") strips
   18 A

Green
   18 C

Dark green
   36 D
   42 E

Blue
   36 D
   42 E

Quilt Top Assembly
1. To make 2 side triangles (H), join 1 (5" x 32") tan strip, 1 (2⅜" x 32") gold strip, and 1 (1⅜" x 32") red strip along long edges as shown in *Cutting Diagram for Piece H.* Align lower edge of pattern piece H with raw edge of red strip. Cut 1 H; move pattern piece and cut second H. Repeat to cut 10 Hs.

2. To make 1 corner triangle, join 1 (1½" x 32") tan strip, 1 (2⅜" x 32") gold strip, and 1 (1⅜" x 32") red strip along long edges as shown in *Cutting Diagram for Piece I.* Align lower edge of pattern piece I with raw edge of red strip. Cut 1 I; move pattern piece and cut second I. Join Is along bias edges, as shown in *Corner Triangle Assembly Diagram.* Repeat to make 4 corner triangles.

3. To make 1 block, fold 1 (8½") tan square in half diagonally; finger-press to form appliqué placement lines. Arrange 1 A, 1 B, and 1 C on tan square as shown in *Block Assembly Diagram;* appliqué pieces to square in alphabetical order. Join 2 blue Ds and 2 dark green Ds to square as shown, mitering corners, to complete 1 block. Repeat to make 18 blocks.

4. Referring to *Quilt Top Assembly Diagram,* join blocks, side triangles, and corner triangles in diagonal rows as shown. Join rows.

5. To make 1 side pieced border, join 12 dark green Es, 11 blue Es, 44 tan Fs, and 4 tan Gs as shown in *Pieced Border Assembly Diagram* and *Quilt Top Assembly Diagram.* Repeat to make second side pieced border. Join to sides of quilt.

To make top border, join 9 dark green Es, 10 blue Es, 36 tan Fs, and 4 tan Gs as shown in *Pieced Border Assembly Diagram* and *Quilt Top Assembly Diagram.* Repeat to make bottom border. Join to quilt, butting corners.

6. Join 1⅜" x 60½" red inner border strips to sides of quilt. Join 1⅜" x 47" red inner border strips to top and bottom of quilt, mitering corners.

7. Join 2¼" x 64" gold outer border strips to sides of quilt. Join 2¼" x 51" gold outer border strips to top and bottom of quilt, mitering corners.

Quilting
Outline-quilt appliquéd pieces, Ds, pieced border, and red inner border. Transfer quilting patterns from pattern pieces H and I to side and corner triangles and quilt. Quilt *Rope Quilting Pattern* (page 75) in gold border.

Finished Edges
Bind with bias binding made from green.

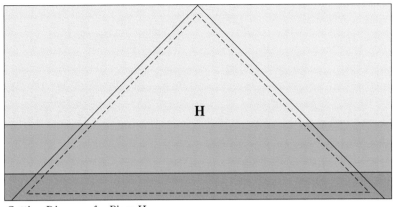

Cutting Diagram for Piece H

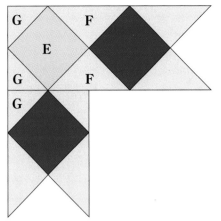

Pieced Border Assembly Diagram

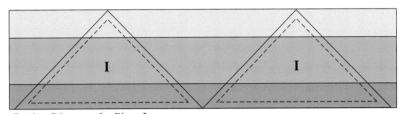

Cutting Diagram for Piece I

Corner Triangle Assembly Diagram

Block Assembly Diagram

Quilt Top Assembly Diagram

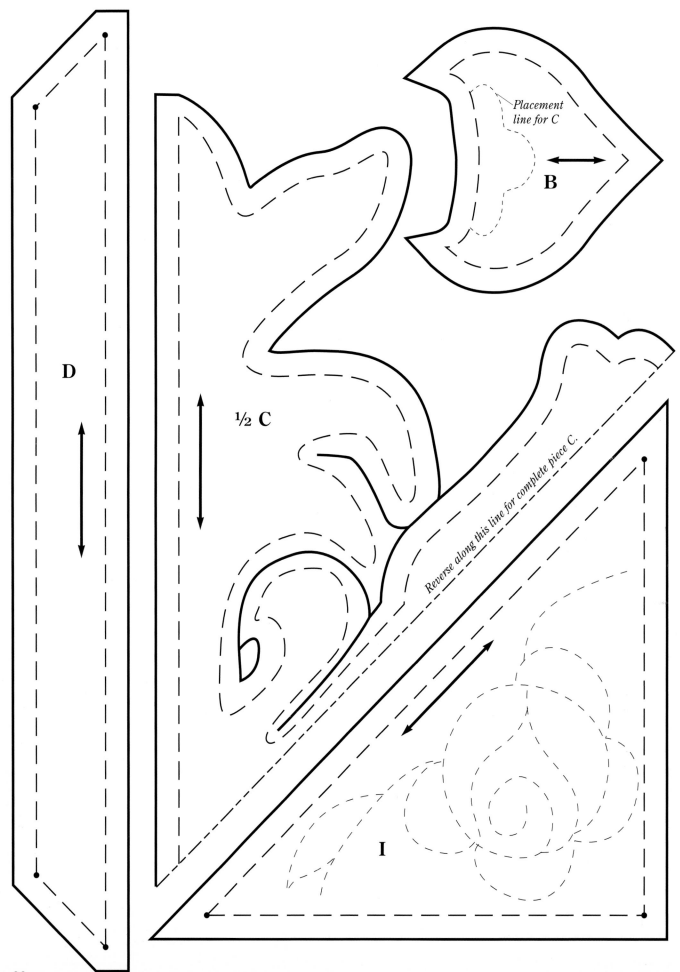

Placement line for C

B

D

½ **C**

Reverse along this line for complete piece C.

I

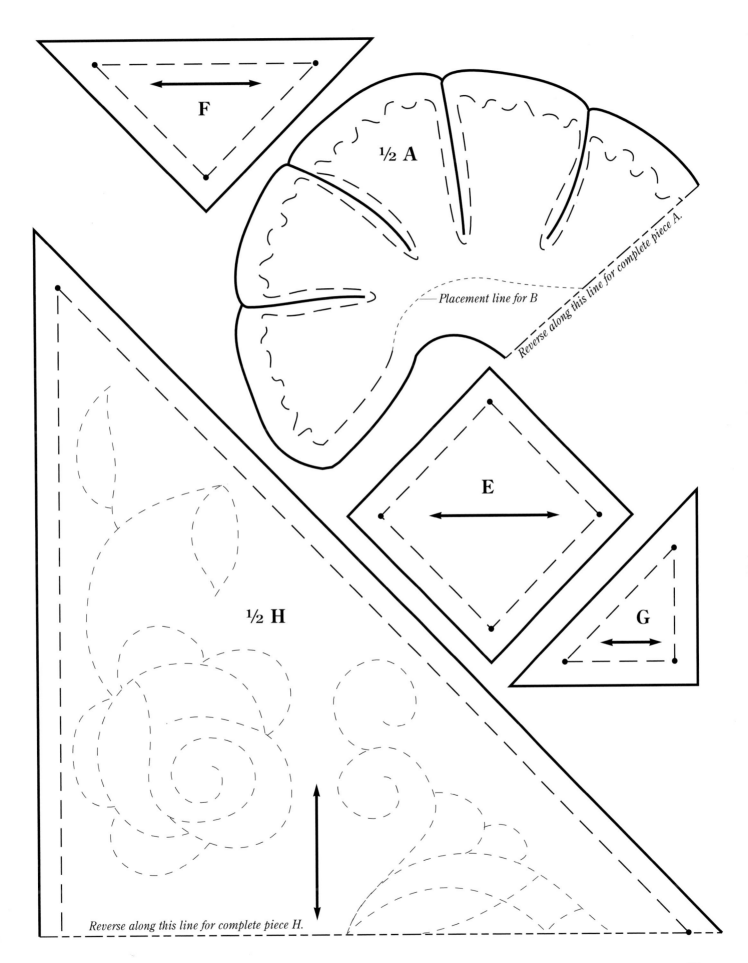

F

½ A

Reverse along this line for complete piece A.

Placement line for B

E

½ H

G

Reverse along this line for complete piece H.

"Hats off to all quilters! Without the inspiration I've received from fellow quilters, I never could have achieved the success I've had."

Christine Kennedy
OAK RIDGE, TENNESSEE

"I've sewed all my life," says Christine Kennedy. "I've made everything from winter coats to bridal gowns." Since her retirement, Christine has had more time to devote to quilting, her favorite sewing activity. Her meticulously pieced, stunning designs have been winning national prizes ever since.

"I hand-piece everything," Christine says. "I want to do it right the first time, so that I won't have to go back later."

Christine looks to many sources for her ideas. "I enjoy looking at quilt magazines and going to quilt shows," she says. "I am amazed at the way the art of quilting has soared in the last decade." Of course, she is still strongly influenced by the woman who got her started in quiltmaking. "I don't want to forget to mention my mother," says Christine. "At 91, she is still piecing quilts and has certainly been an inspiration to me."

Stars with Flaire
1991

Christine worked several hours a day for three years to complete this original design, which contains 2,560 pieces. "The Celtic appliqué around the points of the stars gave them an unusual flair, hence the name *Stars with Flaire*," says Christine. "The quilting inside the bias appliqué was a type of stippling that I had not used before."

Since its completion in 1991, *Stars with Flaire* has won almost every important award offered in quiltmaking. In 1994, Christine won first place in Traditional Pieced Quilts at the American Quilter's Association show in Paducah and first place in the pieced category at the Dollywood Quilt Competition. At the 1993 Smoky Mountain

Quilters' show in Knoxville, *Stars with Flaire* won first place, National Pride in Workmanship, and second place in scrap quilts. It also appeared in a recent issue of *McCall's Quilting* and is featured in *Quilt Art '95 Engagement Calendar,* published by the American Quilter's Society.

Quilt Top Assembly

1. Using entire 2½ yards of floral print, make 1"-wide continuous bias strip. (See "Making Binding," page 143, for instructions.) Cut into 7"-long strips. (You should have about 400 strips). Press under ¼" on each long edge of each strip. Set aside.

2. Referring to *Block Assembly Diagram*, join As as follows: 1 Print 1, 2 Print 2, 3 Print 3, 4 Print 4, 3 Print 5, 2 Print 6, and 1 Print 7, to form 1 diamond. Repeat to make 8 diamonds. Join diamonds.

Transfer bias placement lines to 4 Bs and 4 Cs. Appliqué 1 bias strip along each scallop as shown in *Block Assembly Diagram,* trimming ends of bias strip even with edges of pieces. Join Bs and Cs to diamonds to complete 1 block. Repeat to make 20 blocks.

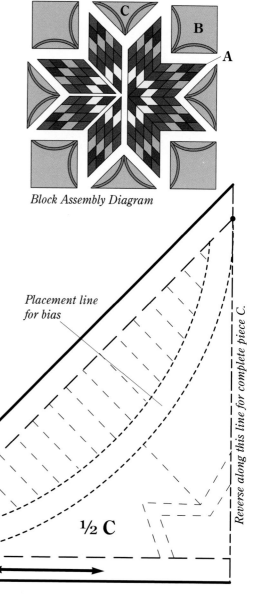

Block Assembly Diagram

Stars with Flaire

Finished Quilt Size
76" x 93"

Number of Blocks and Finished Size
20 blocks   17" x 17"

Fabric Requirements*
Pink	4½ yards
Floral print	2½ yards
Print 1	20 (9") squares
Print 2	20 (12") squares
Print 3	20 (12") squares
Print 4	20 (18") squares
Print 5	20 (12") squares
Print 6	20 (12") squares
Print 7	20 (9") squares
Backing	6 yards
Pink for bias binding	1 yard

*Prints are numbered from center of star outward.

Pieces to Cut**
Pink
  2 (4½" x 93½") border strips
  2 (4½" x 76½") border strips
  80 B
  80 C
Print 1
  160 A (8 of each)
Print 2
  320 A (16 of each)
Print 3
  480 A (24 of each)
Print 4
  640 A (32 of each)
Print 5
  480 A (24 of each)
Print 6
  320 A (16 of each)
Print 7
  160 A (8 of each)

**For floral print, see Step 1.

Placement line for bias

½ C

Reverse along this line for complete piece C.

3. Join blocks in 5 rows of 4 blocks each. Join rows.

4. To make 1 side border, transfer bias placement lines from *Border Quilting Pattern* to 1 (4½" x 93½") pink border strip. Appliqué 1 bias strip along each scallop, trimming ends of bias strips even with edges of border. Repeat to make second side border. Join to sides of quilt.

In same manner, appliqué bias strips to remaining border strips. Join to top and bottom of quilt, mitering corners.

Quilting

Transfer quilting patterns from pattern pieces B and C; quilt. Quilt *Border Quilting Pattern* in borders.

Finished Edges

Bind with bias binding made from pink.

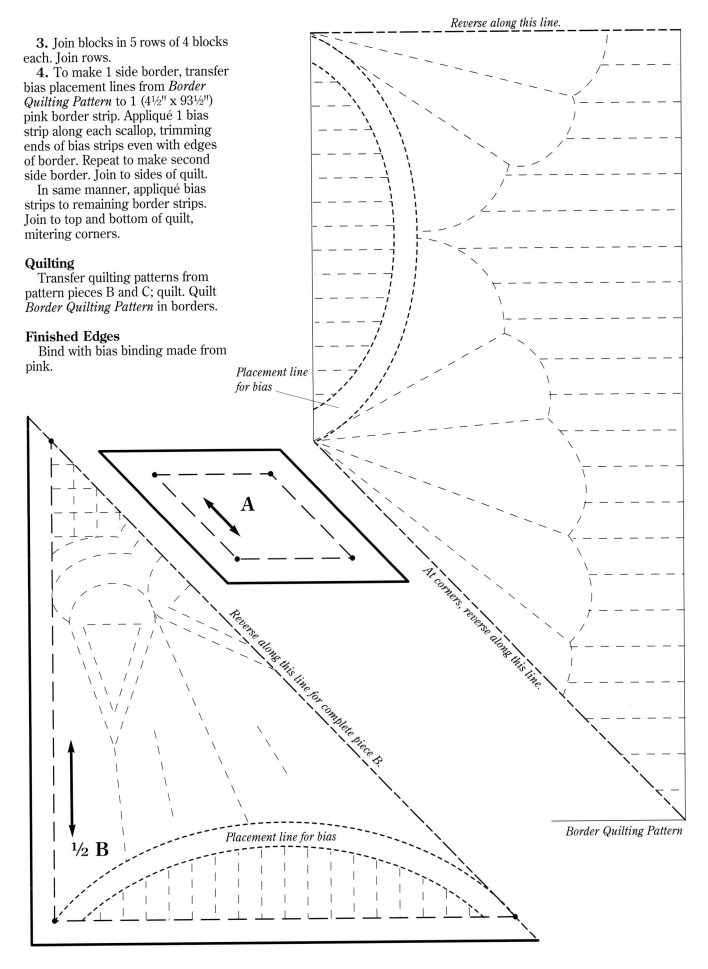

Reverse along this line.

Placement line for bias

At corners, reverse along this line.

Border Quilting Pattern

A

Reverse along this line for complete piece B.

½ B

Placement line for bias

*"When I tell someone I'm a quilter,
I say it with a lot of pride!"*

Rosemary Youngs
WALKER, MICHIGAN

Preschool teacher Rosemary Youngs looks to the 1930s for her ideas, enjoying appliquéing and hand-quilting pieces with the look of that era. Five years ago, Rosemary began quilting by making bed coverings and baby quilts for each of her four children, using traditional patterns such as Trip Around the World and Irish Chain. It was only two years ago that she began to appliqué, yet her intricate *American Quilters and Their Quilts* drew appreciative crowds at the 1995 American Quilter's Society show in Paducah.

"There is a certain beauty you can create using appliqué," says Rosemary. "The flowers seem to come alive and the butterflies appear to be flying."

Rosemary's Butterflies
1994

Rosemary collected all of the vintage fabrics for this quilt from estate sales. She began her design with a traditional tulip pattern in the center but quickly saw that the butterflies were needed to balance the block. "Every time I appliquéd another butterfly," Rosemary says, "I would just stand back and admire the fabric. It reminds me of quilts my grandmothers would have made if they had been quilters."

Rosemary actually made this quilt for her 10-year-old daughter, Amy. The quilt is displayed in their living room, and Amy takes great pleasure in telling guests that the quilt is hers. "I know she will always cherish and love it," Rosemary says. "And that's what quilts are for!"

On the back of one of the blocks, Rosemary appliquéd a tulip and four butterflies. Across two of the leaves, she wrote her name and "My first appliqué quilt." The messages on the butterflies read as follows:
Upper left (white): "Dear Amy, When this you see, Remember me! Love, Mom"
Upper right (orange): "This quilt was especially made for Amy Beth Youngs who seems to enjoy the simple pleasures in life such as butterflies."
Lower right (purple): "The fabric that was used to make this quilt was purchased at an estate sale and is authentic fabric from the 1930s."
Lower left (yellow): "This butterfly quilt was started in the fall of 1993 and finished in May of 1994. It took approximately 9 months to appliqué it and quilt it."

Quilt Top Assembly

1. Cut 1 (14") square from butcher paper; fold square into quarters horizontally and vertically. Using ruler and pencil, draw quarter-circle with 7" radius on butcher paper. Cut along line and unfold to make paper circle with 14" diameter. Fold 1 white square into quarters diagonally; finger-press. Unfold. Aligning center of butcher paper circle with center of white square, lightly mark circle on fabric. Remove paper. Mark second circle ¼" outside of first. Repeat to mark remaining squares.

2. Referring to *¼ Block Appliqué Placement Diagram*, arrange 4 blue Bs, 4 Cs, 4 Ds, and 1 E along placement lines of 1 white square as shown. Appliqué pieces to square in alphabetical order. Arrange 4 butterflies (A) on marked circles at diagonal placement lines; appliqué to complete 1 block. Repeat to make 5 blocks. In same manner, make 4 blocks using pink Bs.

3. Alternating blocks with blue and pink Bs as shown in photograph, join blocks into 3 rows of 3 blocks each. Join rows.

4. From 15" green square, make 130" of ¾"-wide continuous bias strip. Fold under ¼" on each long edge; press.

5. To make top border, fold 1 (10½" x 57½") white strip in half vertically to find center; finger-press. Referring to *½ Border Appliqué Placement Diagram*, lightly mark position of vine. Appliqué bias vine to border strip, following marked lines. Arrange 2 pink Bs, 2 Cs, 8 Ds, 1 E, 2 pink Fs, 2 blue Fs, and 4 Gs as shown in *½ Border Appliqué Placement Diagram*. Appliqué pieces to border in alphabetical order. Repeat to make bottom border. Join to top and bottom of quilt.

6. In same manner, make 1 side border using 2 blue Bs, 2 Cs, 8 Ds, 1 E, 2 pink Fs, 2 blue Fs, and 4 Gs. Repeat to make second side border. Join to sides of quilt, butting corners.

Quilting

Outline-quilt around all appliquéd pieces. Quilt circles on marked lines. Inside circles, quilt ½" cross-hatch pattern. Quilt *Corner Feather Plume Quilting Pattern* in corner of each block. In borders, quilt vertical lines, ½" apart, as shown in photograph.

Rosemary's Butterflies

Finished Quilt Size
77" x 77"

Number of Blocks and Finished Size
9 blocks   19" x 19"

Fabric Requirements
White	4¾ yards
Green	1¼ yards
Pink	¼ yard
Blue	¼ yard
Pastel prints	1 yard
Backing	5 yards
White for bias binding	1 yard

Pieces to Cut
White
    2 (10½" x 77½") border strips
    2 (10½" x 57½") border strips
    9 (19½") squares
Green
    15" square for bias vines
    44 C
    68 D
    13 E
    16 G
Pink
    20 B
    8 F
Blue
    24 B
    8 F
Pastel prints
    36 A

Other Materials
Butcher paper
Ruler (at least 8" long)

Finished Edges
Bind with bias binding made from white.

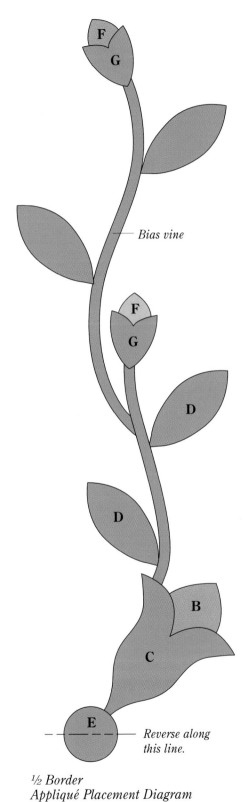

Bias vine

½ Border
Appliqué Placement Diagram

Reverse along this line.

Reverse along this line.

Reverse along this line.

E D

C

B

A

Appliqué
placement line

¼ Block Appliqué Placement Diagram

F
G

F
G

D

D

B

C

E

Reverse along
this line.

Quilt Top Assembly Diagram

105

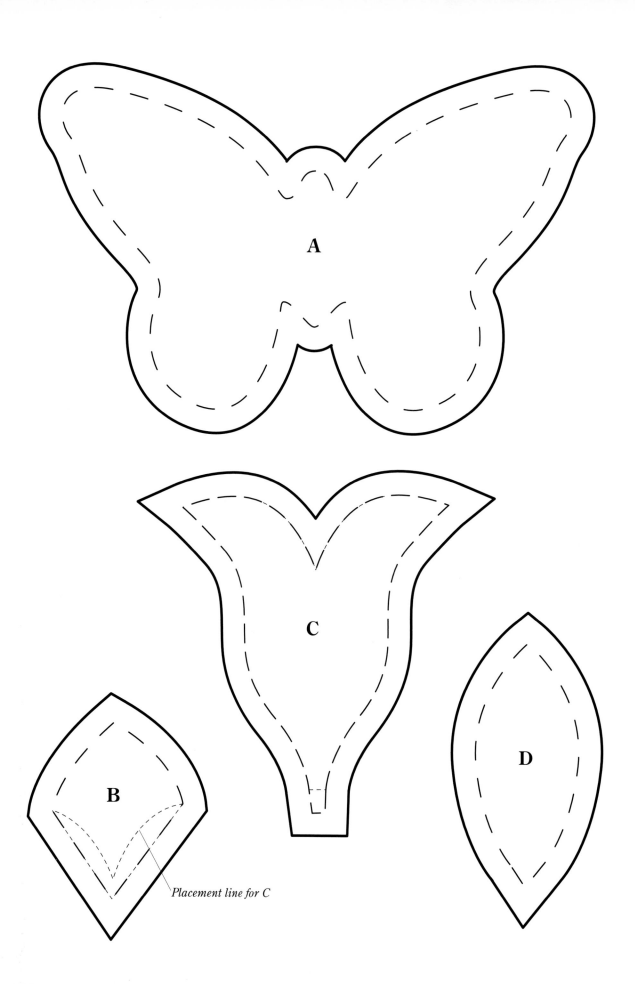

A

C

B

Placement line for C

D

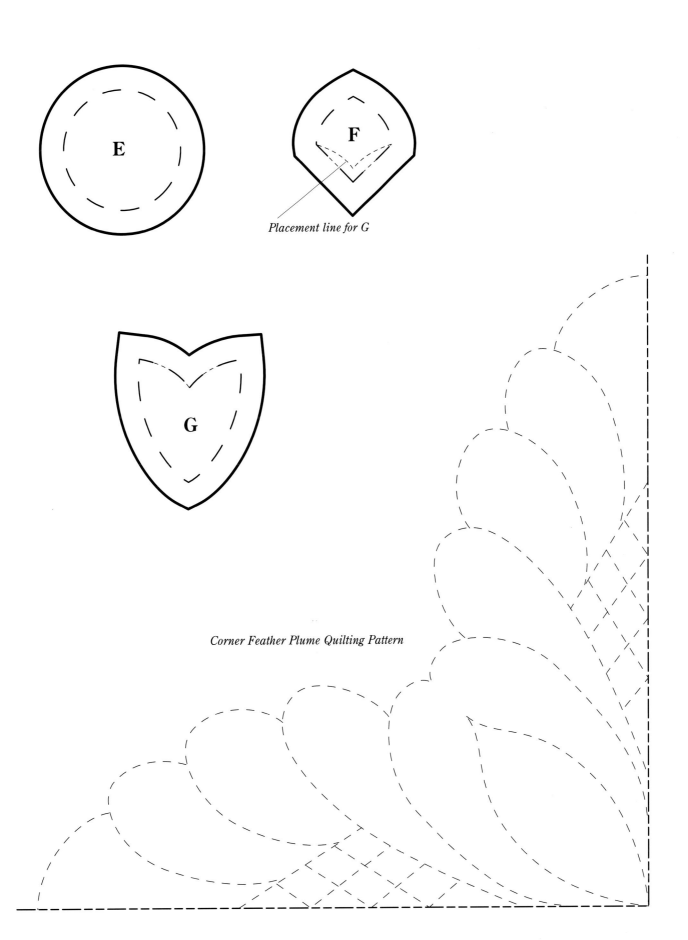

E

F

Placement line for G

G

Corner Feather Plume Quilting Pattern

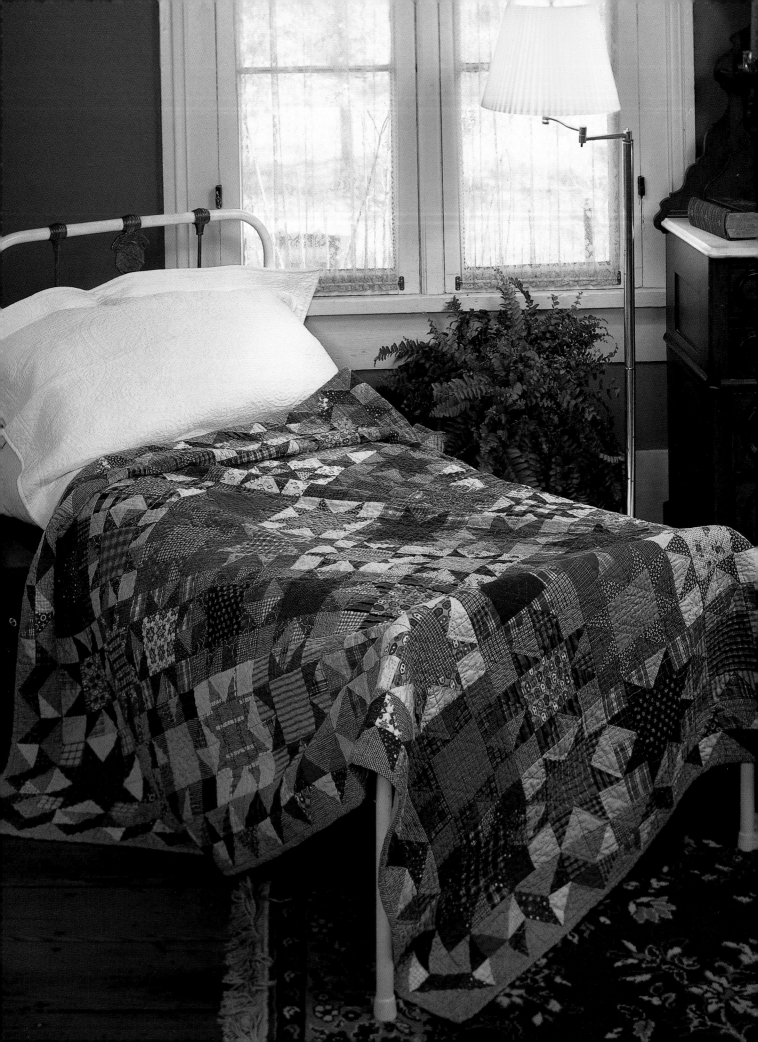

Nancy M. Jackson
NEW BRITAIN, PENNSYLVANIA

In 1980, Nancy Jackson finished her first quilt, a 20-block crazy quilt backed with white velvet. "I was terribly sentimental about that quilt," Nancy says. "I used old family fabric—silks, velvets, brocades used by my mother and grandmother, and woolens from my childhood clothing." Nancy planned to use that quilt in her bedroom, but the sunny, south-facing room proved too much for the fragile old silks, and the quilt began to disintegrate almost immediately.

After that disappointment, Nancy set quilting aside for a decade. She stenciled, painted, and embroidered fabric, but quilting continued to tug at her. "I owe the discovery of my true avocation to the Plumstead Christian Quilters," she says. This group of quilting friends encouraged her and helped her improve her skills. "One afternoon, they gently told me that you don't leave your knots on top!" Nancy says, smiling.

So far, Nancy has found herself staying with traditional patterns, although she is experimenting with contemporary designs. "I am still trying everything," she says. "I haven't yet found the single direction I will take."

An American Collage
1994

Nancy loves old fabrics and inherited many vintage fabrics, the oldest dating to the 1830s, from her husband's grandmother. A contest asking for quilts made from squares and half-square triangles sparked the idea for *An American Collage*. "I knew I could make a variable star quilt with my assorted fabrics," says Nancy. "I hand-pieced for five months.

I have another 48 blocks that I rejected because they weren't perfect enough or the colors weren't pleasing."

The contest Nancy had hoped to enter was canceled, but she liked the quilt and thought it had merit. She entered it in the 1994 Pennsylvania National Quilt Extravaganza in Fort Washington, a judged show with the theme "From Sea to Shining Sea."

And when the 1995 Williamsburg Quilt Festival announced its theme of "Family Influences on Creativity," Nancy knew she had to enter *An American Collage* in that show as well. "I learned to covet important scraps," Nancy said in her theme statement. "I learned not to pass up a lovely piece. I recycle, I conserve."

Quilt Top Assembly

1. Referring to *Block Assembly Diagram,* join 4 As and 8 Bs of background fabric, 8 scrap Bs, and 1 scrap C as shown to make 1 block. Repeat to make 72 blocks.

2. Arrange blocks in 9 rows of 8 blocks each. Join blocks. Join rows.

3. To make 1 side border, join 72 Bs of background fabric and 72 scrap Bs as shown in *Quilt Top Assembly Diagram.* Repeat to make second side border. Join to sides of quilt.

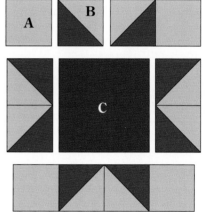

Block Assembly Diagram

An American Collage

Finished Quilt Size
72" x 80"

Number of Blocks and Finished Size
72 blocks   8" x 8"

Fabric Requirements
Background fabric	4¼ yards
Scraps for stars and borders	2¾ yards
Scraps for centers of stars	1½ yards
Backing	5 yards
Blue for bias binding	¾ yard

Pieces to Cut
Background fabric
  288 A
  852 B
  4 D
Scraps for stars and borders
  860 B
Scraps for centers of stars
  72 C

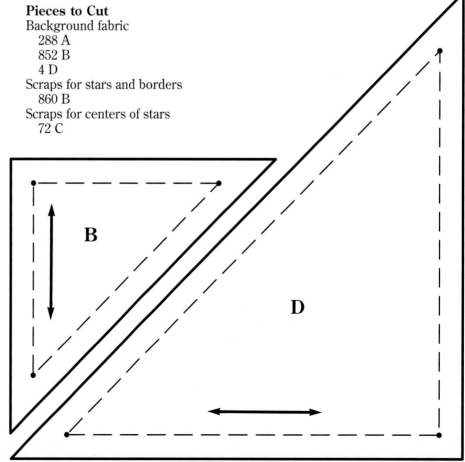

4. To make top border, join 66 Bs and 2 Ds of background fabric and 70 scrap Bs as shown in *Pieced Border Assembly Diagram* and *Quilt Top Assembly Diagram.* Repeat to make bottom border. Join to quilt, butting corners.

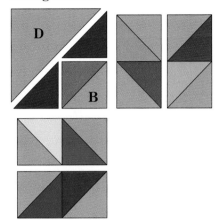

Pieced Border Assembly Diagram

Quilting
Quilt concentric squares in centers of Cs as shown on pattern piece. Quilt remainder in-the-ditch, or quilt as desired.

Finished Edges
Bind with bias binding made from blue.

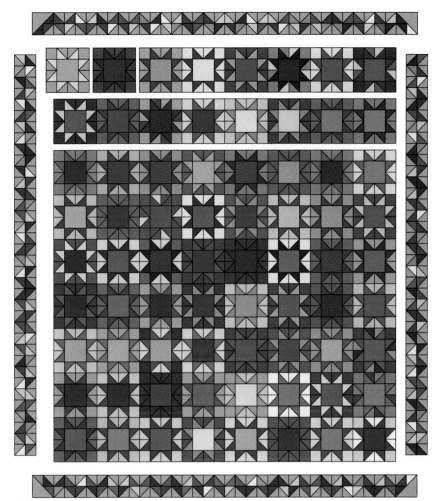

Quilt Top Assembly Diagram

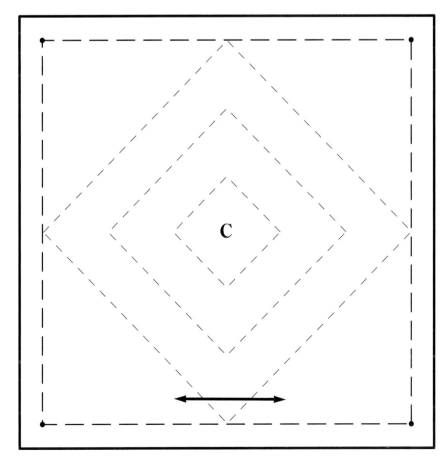

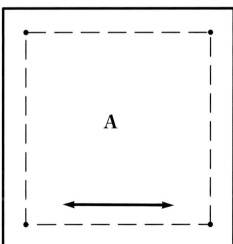

Bee Quilters

Button Berries

Prairie Storm

Sadie's Choice

Front row, from left: Carol Williamson, Jamis Kresyman, Debbie Duane, Patti Connor, Sarah White, Joan Bement. Back row, from left: Drew Benage, Martha Haertling, Ponnie Brinkman, Mary Olson, Jean Ameduri, Joyce Mottern, Frank Foley, Judy Leubke, Diane Terwestern, Jana Shepard, Connie Ewbank.

Thimble & Thread Quilt Guild of Greater St. Louis
ST. LOUIS, MISSOURI

The Thimble & Thread Quilt Guild of Greater St. Louis is a diverse group of 270 members who live in and near St. Louis. "We do a lot of regular guild stuff," says Patti Connor, guild member and the designer of *Button Berries*. "We make many quilts for the community—for hospitals, the Ronald McDonald House, and the local AIDS outreach."

One of the guild's favorite activities is their yearly trip to the American Quilter's Society show in Paducah. The members charter a bus and wear T-shirts with the guild's name and logo. "We enjoy the trip as much as the show," Patti says. "It's a time we can spend quilting and talking as we ride."

Button Berries
1995

Button Berries was designed by Patti Connor as a group fundraising project for the members of the Thimble & Thread Quilt Guild. Each member made a block, with the more skilled members choosing the challenging blocks and the beginners piecing the simple five-patch blocks. Patti completed the quilt, finishing the binding in an all-out effort to have the quilt ready in time for this book.

Although the original design called for appliquéd circles for the berries, Patti suggested that the members use buttons from a favorite shirt or dress in order to add a personal touch.

"This is a good design for a group project," Patti says. "Not only are different skill levels represented, but different techniques as well. Almost any quilter can find a block suitable to her interests and abilities."

Button Berries

Finished Quilt Size
80" x 100"

Number of Blocks and Finished Size
63 blocks   10" x 10"

Fabric Requirements
Off-white	1½ yards
Light beige	5 yards
Dark beige	1 yard
Navy print	⅛ yard
Navy plaid	½ yard
Navy stripe	¾ yard
Green	1⅛ yards
Backing	7¾ yards
Navy stripe for bias binding	1 yard

Other Materials
White pearl buttons, various sizes

Pieces to Cut
Off-white
   288 A

Light beige
   2 (5½" x 100½") border strips
   2 (5½ x 80½") border strips
   15 (10½") squares
   100 A
   12 B
   100 C
   12 D
Dark beige
   44 A
   44 C
Navy print
   16 A
Navy plaid
   20 B
   16 C
Navy stripe
   20 D
   16 E
Green
   1 (18") square for bias stems
   44 F
   44 G

Quilt Top Assembly
1. Referring to *Block 1 Assembly Diagram,* join 9 off-white As, 4 light beige As, and 4 light beige Cs as shown to complete 1 Block 1. Repeat to make 8 Block 1s.

2. Referring to *Block 2 Assembly Diagram,* join 9 off-white As, 2 light beige As, 2 light beige Cs, 2 dark beige As, and 2 dark beige Cs as shown to complete 1 Block 2. Repeat to make 20 Block 2s.

3. Referring to *Block 3 Assembly Diagram,* join 9 off-white As, 3 light beige As, 3 light beige Cs, 1 dark beige A, and 1 dark beige C as shown to complete 1 Block 3. Repeat to make 4 Block 3s.

4. Referring to *Block 4 Assembly Diagram,* join 1 light beige A, 1 light beige B, 1 light beige C, 1 light beige D, 1 navy print A, 1 navy plaid B, 1 navy plaid C, 1 navy stripe D, and 1 navy stripe E as shown to complete 1 Block 4. Repeat to make 12 Block 4s.

5. Referring to *Block 5 Assembly Diagram,* join 1 light beige A, 1 light beige C, 1 navy print A, 2 navy plaid Bs, 1 navy plaid C, 2 navy stripe Ds, and 1 navy stripe E as shown to complete 1 Block 5. Repeat to make 4 Block 5s.

6. From green 18" square, make 204" of 1⅛"-wide continuous bias strip. Cut strip into 2 (12"-long) and 12 (15"-long) strips. Fold under ¼" on each long edge of each strip; press.

7. To make 1 Block 6, lightly mark 1 (10½") light beige square, using Bias Guide for Block 6 on page 118 and referring to *Block 6 Appliqué Placement Diagram.* Appliqué 1 (12"-long) bias strip to square, following marked lines. Trim ends of bias even with edge of square. Referring to *Block 6 Appliqué Placement Diagram,* appliqué 2 Fs and 2 Gs to square as shown to complete 1 Block 6. Repeat to make 2 Block 6s.

8. In same manner, appliqué 1 (15"-long) bias strip to 1 (10½") light beige square, using Bias Guide for Block 7 on page 118 and referring to *Block 7 Appliqué Placement Diagram.* Appliqué 3 Fs and 3 Gs to square as shown to complete 1 Block 7. Repeat to make 12 Block 7s.

9. To make 1 Block 8, appliqué 4 Fs and 4 Gs around center of 1 (10½") light beige square as shown in *Block 8 Appliqué Placement Diagram.*

10. Referring to *Quilt Top Assembly Diagram* for placement, join blocks in 9 rows of 7 blocks each. Join rows.

11. Join 5½" x 100½" light beige border strips to sides of quilt. Join 5½" x 80½" light beige border strips to top and bottom of quilt, mitering corners.

Quilting

Outline-quilt edges of appliquéd pieces and bias strips. Quilt remainder of blocks in diagonal lines through centers of As. (See photograph.) Quilt borders in parallel lines, 2" apart.

Referring to *Block 6, 7, and 8 Appliqué Placement Diagrams,* stitch buttons to quilt to form berries.

Finished Edges

Bind with bias binding made from navy stripe.

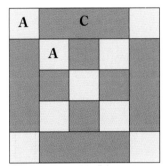

Block 1 Assembly Diagram—Make 8.

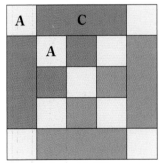

Block 2 Assembly Diagram—Make 20.

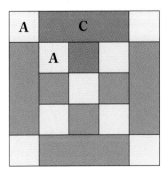

Block 3 Assembly Diagram—Make 4.

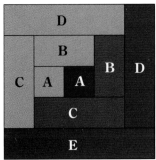

Block 4 Assembly Diagram—Make 12.

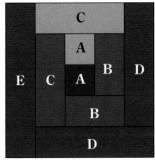

Block 5 Assembly Diagram—Make 4.

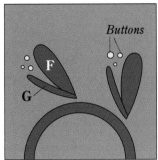

Block 6 Appliqué Placement Diagram—Make 2.

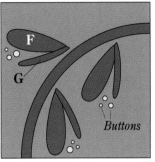

Block 7 Appliqué Placement Diagram—Make 12.

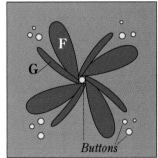

Block 8 Appliqué Placement Diagram—Make 1.

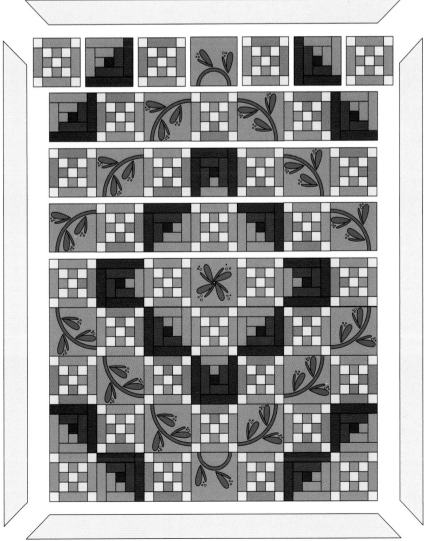

Quilt Top Assembly Diagram

117

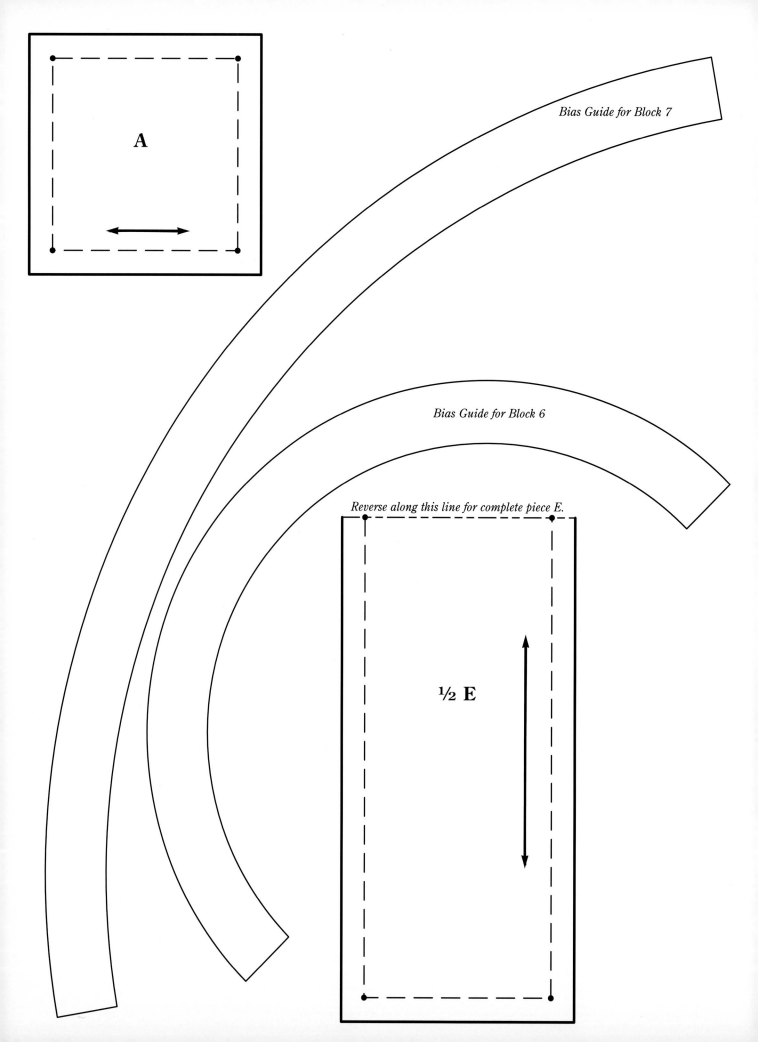

A

Bias Guide for Block 7

Bias Guide for Block 6

Reverse along this line for complete piece E.

½ E

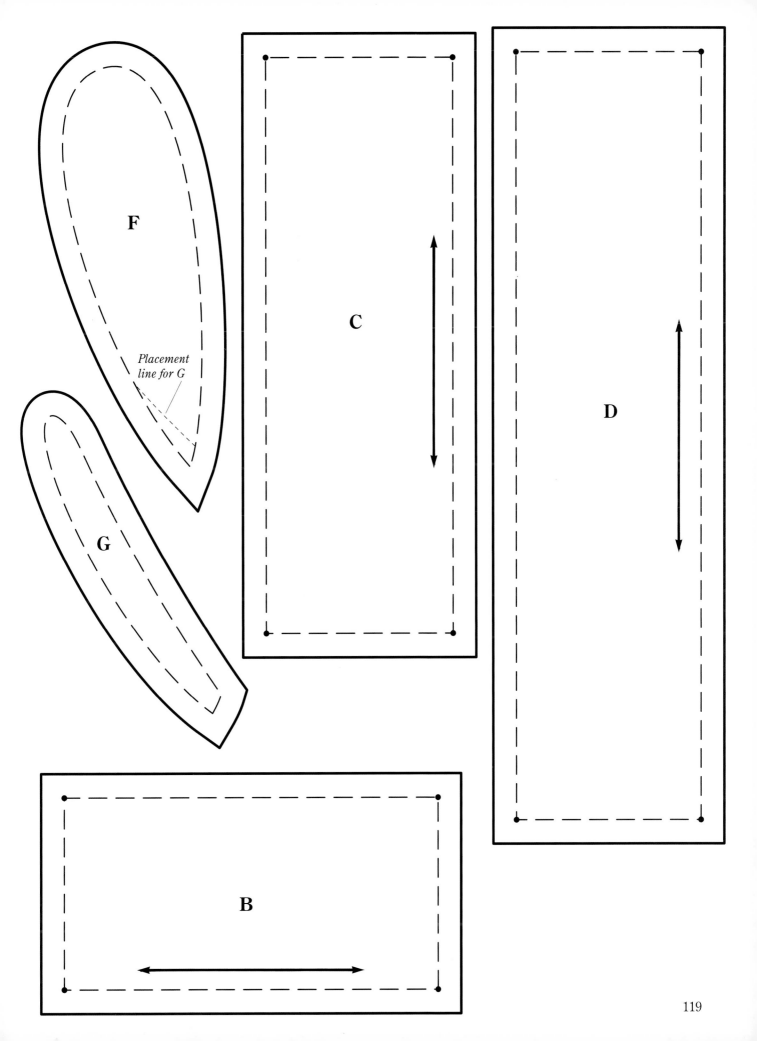

F

C

D

Placement line for G

G

B

119

"Prairie Storm was a great lesson in compromise; none of us have the same color preferences!"

From left: Sue Cooley, Jean Ahlm, Candy Breitenfeldt, Gloria Jones, Lynn Sedlacek, Robin Wolberson, Kim Strange.

The Cut-ups
CHIPPEWA FALLS, WISCONSIN

The Cut-ups are a young quilting group who began meeting in the fall of 1991. "We met each other through the Chippewa Valley Newcomers Club," says spokesman Gloria Jones, "where we served on a fund-raising committee." Their first project was a quilt raffle. "The raffle was a success and our group just couldn't stop quilting!" says Gloria.

Because they are an informal and relatively inexperienced group, Gloria says that learning of their acceptance for this year's *Great American Quilts* was a surprise, even though a pleasant one. "To celebrate," she says, "we had cake and champagne at our first guild meeting after being told we would be in the book. Wish you could have been here!"

Prairie Storm
1994

When Gloria bought a copy of *Great American Quilts 1994*, she found inside the book a newsletter inviting readers to participate in a quilt challenge. Gloria asked the other members if they were interested in designing a quilt using only the pattern pieces provided in the challenge, and the Cut-ups set to work enthusiastically.

After considering a number of traditional blocks that used the given templates, they selected several and began playing with the layout. Next came color selection, which involved a road trip to the Calico Shoppe in Eau Claire, a town 12 miles south of Chippewa Falls.

"This quilt was a great lesson in compromise," Gloria says, "as none of the seven members have the same color preferences!"

After much work, the group finished and bound *Prairie Storm* in August of 1994. As sometimes happens when one project is the work of many hands, the quilt would not lie flat. "Several members took out the binding and all the quilting from the edges up to the Oklahoma Twister blocks," Gloria says. "During the quilting some of the backing had been stretched a lot." After much reworking, the quilt was *really* completed in September.

"The binding is now flat. The quilt is now done," Gloria says. And with a smile, she adds, "Although we were thrilled to be chosen, this is *not* an annual project!"

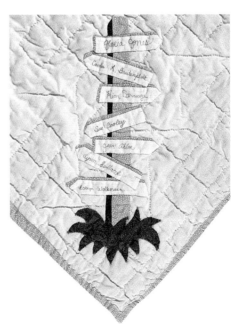

True to their individual natures, the quilters who form the Cut-ups stitched themselves into the quilt's backing as signposts pointing every which way!

121

Prairie Storm

Finished Quilt Size
72" x 72"

Number of Blocks and Finished Size
36 blocks   12" x 12"

Fabric Requirements
White	1¾ yards
Light teal	1½ yards
Dark teal	¾ yard
Beige	2½ yards
Brown	1½ yards
Backing	4½ yards
Beige for bias binding	¾ yard

Pieces to Cut
White
   4 A
   304 C
   140 D
Light teal
   16 B
   480 C
Dark teal
   192 C
Beige
   464 C
   116 D
Brown
   352 C
   96 D

Quilt Top Assembly
1. Referring to *Weathervane Block Assembly Diagram,* join 1 white A, 4 light teal Bs, 8 light teal Cs, 16 beige Cs, 8 brown Cs, 4 beige Ds, and 4 brown Ds as shown to make 1 Weathervane block. Repeat to make 4 Weathervane blocks.

2. Referring to *Oklahoma Twister Block 1 Assembly Diagram,* join 12 white Cs, 16 dark teal Cs, 4 beige Cs, 15 white Ds, and 5 beige Ds to make 1 Oklahoma Twister Block 1. Repeat to make 4 Oklahoma Twister Block 1s.

Referring to *Oklahoma Twister Block 2 Assembly Diagram,* join 8 white Cs, 16 dark teal Cs, 8 beige Cs, 10 white Ds, and 10 beige Ds to make 1 Oklahoma Twister Block 2. Repeat to make 8 Oklahoma Twister Block 2s.

3. Referring to *Star Twist Block 1 Assembly Diagram,* join 16 white Cs, 16 light teal Cs, 16 beige Cs, 16 brown Cs, and 4 brown Ds to make 1 Star Twist Block 1. Repeat to make 4 Star Twist Block 1s.

Referring to *Star Twist Block 2 Assembly Diagram,* join 8 white Cs, 24 light teal Cs, 16 beige Cs, 16 brown Cs, and 4 brown Ds to make 1 Star Twist Block 2. Repeat to make 16 Star Twist Block 2s.

4. Referring to *Quilt Top Assembly Diagram,* join Weathervane blocks in 2 rows of 2 blocks each to form center.

Arrange Oklahoma Twister blocks to form border around center, placing Oklahoma Twister Block 1s at corners and Oklahoma Twister Block 2s along sides. Join to sides of quilt.

Arrange Star Twist blocks to form outer border as shown in *Quilt Top Assembly Diagram,* placing Star Twist Block 1s at corners and Star Twist Block 2s along sides. Join to sides of quilt.

Quilting
   Quilt in-the-ditch around each piece, or quilt as desired.

Finished Edges
   Bind with bias binding made from beige.

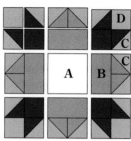

Weathervane Block Assembly Diagram—Make 4.

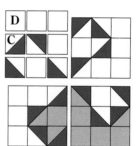

Oklahoma Twister Block 1 Assembly Diagram—Make 4.

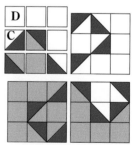

Oklahoma Twister Block 2 Assembly Diagram—Make 8.

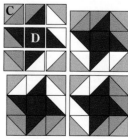

Star Twist Block 1 Assembly Diagram—Make 4.

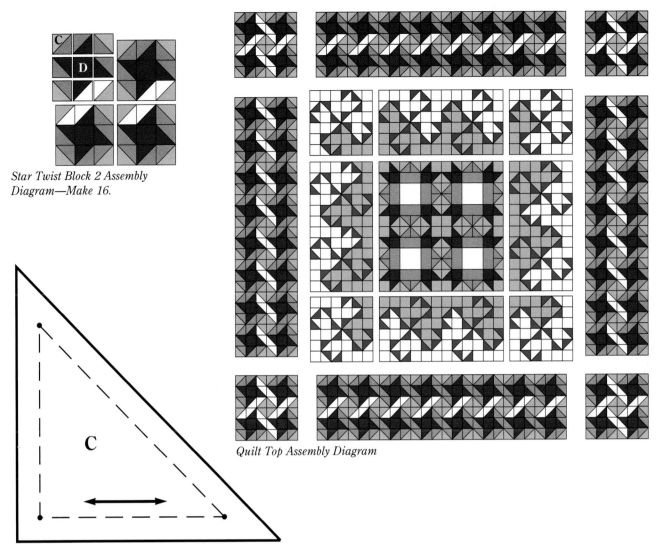

Star Twist Block 2 Assembly Diagram—Make 16.

C

D

Quilt Top Assembly Diagram

C

A

D

B

Front row, from left: Nancy Adams, Carrie Capek, Blanche Young, Angie Bissell. Back row, from left: Marie M. Fischer, Nancy Taylor, Jackie Osterman, Diane Fennessey, Mary Caltigirone, Devi Harjani, Reba Taylor, Virginia Byers, Theresa Freker, Linda Jones, Olive Gratton, Nancy Popham. Not pictured: Ruth Sheen, Doris Perrette, Eve Levine.

Krazy Quilters Club
TEMPLE TERRACE, FLORIDA

Each Tuesday morning at 10:00, president Marie Fischer calls the roll of The Krazy Quilters Club. "That's about as structured as we get," she says. "Our founder, Sadie Bell, wanted a relaxed atmosphere so no one would feel uneasy."

During meetings, members may work on their own projects or work on club quilts—a tool Marie says they use to teach new members the art of quiltmaking. "A member must work on two club quilts and then is eligible to win the next club quilt," she says. "In turn, the winning member is in charge of the next club project."

The Krazy Quilters Club makes many quilts for "at risk" babies in local hospitals. They have also made a historical quilt honoring their city that they donated to the public library, where everyone can enjoy it.

"Oh, yes," Marie adds. "Two or three times a year, we work in a covered-dish luncheon so that we can show off our cooking talents, too. It's funny how attendance always goes up for those meetings!"

Sadie's Choice
1994

To honor their founder, Sadie C. Bell, on her 85th birthday, the Krazy Quilters Club made a special *Sadie's Choice* quilt. "Sadie inspired hundreds of ladies, young and old, to become interested in quilting," says Marie Fischer.

Sadie started the club in 1977. Even though she had to leave Temple Terrace in 1985, she encouraged Marie to keep the club going. Along with the quilt, members made Sadie a matching pillow. On the back of the pillow, they included a special surprise: photographs from the club's founding and pictures of some of their famous covered-dish luncheons printed on the fabric backing.

Sadie's Choice won first place at the 1995 Florida State Fair and at the 1995 Strawberry Festival in Plant City, Florida.

Quilt Top Assembly

1. To make 1 corner trapezoid (J), fold 1 (9"-wide) pink strip in half vertically to find center; finger-press. From center line, measure along top and bottom edges as shown in *Cutting Diagram for Piece J;* mark. Draw lines to connect marked points. Cut along lines; discard ends. Repeat to make second J.

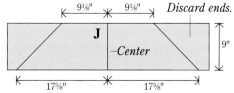

Cutting Diagram for Piece J

2. To make 1 block, fold 1 (17½") pink square in half horizontally, vertically, and diagonally. Finger-press fold lines to form appliqué placement lines. Unfold. Referring to *Block Appliqué Placement Diagram,* appliqué 4 Hs, 4 Gs, 4 Fs, and 4 Es to square in that order. Join 12 Cs and 12 Ds alternately to make ring as shown. Appliqué outer edge of ring to center of square. Appliqué 1 B and 1 A to center of square, in that order, to complete 1 block. Repeat to make 12 blocks. Set remaining 17½" squares aside for setting squares.

Sadie's Choice

Finished Quilt Size
96" x 120"

Number of Blocks and Finished Size
12 blocks   17" x 17"

Fabric Requirements

Pink	9 yards
Gold	½ yard
Black floral	1¼ yards
Dark pink	1½ yards
White floral	1 yard
Teal	1¾ yards
Backing	9 yards
Black floral for bias binding	1 yard

Pieces to Cut

Pink
  2 (9"-wide) crosswise strips*
  28 (17½") squares
  3 (25¼") squares**
Gold
  40 A
Black floral
  12 B
  48 E
Dark pink
  188 D
  48 F
  48 H
White floral
  144 C
  12 K
Teal
  48 G
  116 I
  12 L

*See Step 1.
**Cut each square into quarters diagonally for 11 side triangles. (You will have 1 left over.)

Block Appliqué Placement Diagram

3. From black floral, make 450" of 1"-wide continuous bias for vines for side triangles. (See "Making Binding," page 143, for instructions.) Cut into 12 (30"-long) strips and 2 (45"-long) strips. Fold under ¼" on each long edge of each strip; press.

4. Referring to *Side Triangle Appliqué Placement Diagram,* appliqué 1 (30"-long) bias strip to 1 side triangle as shown. Appliqué 2 As, 4 Ds, and 8 Is to triangle as shown to complete 1 triangle. Repeat to make 11 triangles.

5. Referring to *Corner Appliqué Placement Diagram,* appliqué 1 (45"-long) bias strip to 1 J as shown. Appliqué 3 As and 14 Is as shown to complete corner. Repeat to make 2 corners.

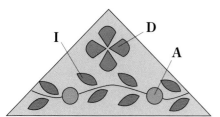

Side Triangle Appliqué Placement Diagram

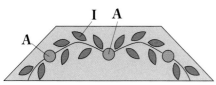

Corner Appliqué Placement Diagram

6. Join blocks, setting squares, side triangles, and corners in diagonal rows as shown in *Quilt Top Assembly Diagram.* Join rows.

7. Referring to *Quilt Top Assembly Diagram* and photograph for placement, appliqué 1 K and 1 L, in that order, to corners of setting squares between side triangles.

Quilting

Outline-quilt around all appliquéd pieces. If desired, echo-quilt ¼" outside of outline quilting. In setting squares, quilt *Heart Wreath Quilting Pattern.*

Finished Edges

Bind with bias binding made from black floral.

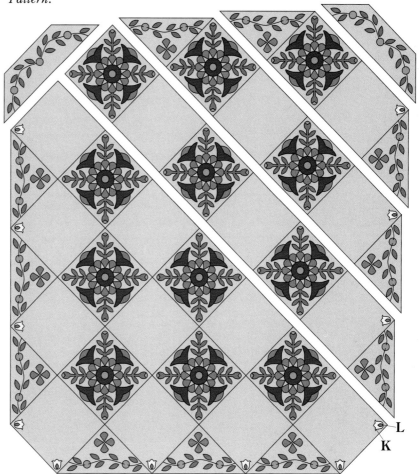

Quilt Top Assembly Diagram

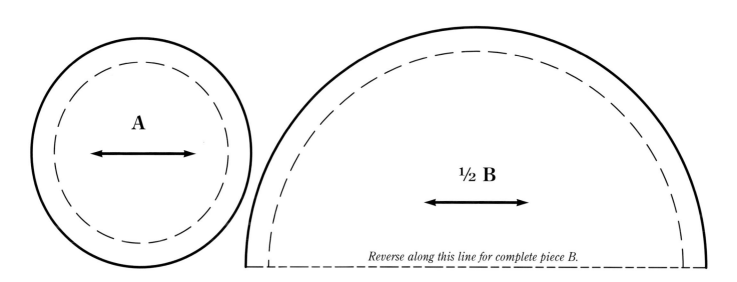

Reverse along this line for complete piece B.

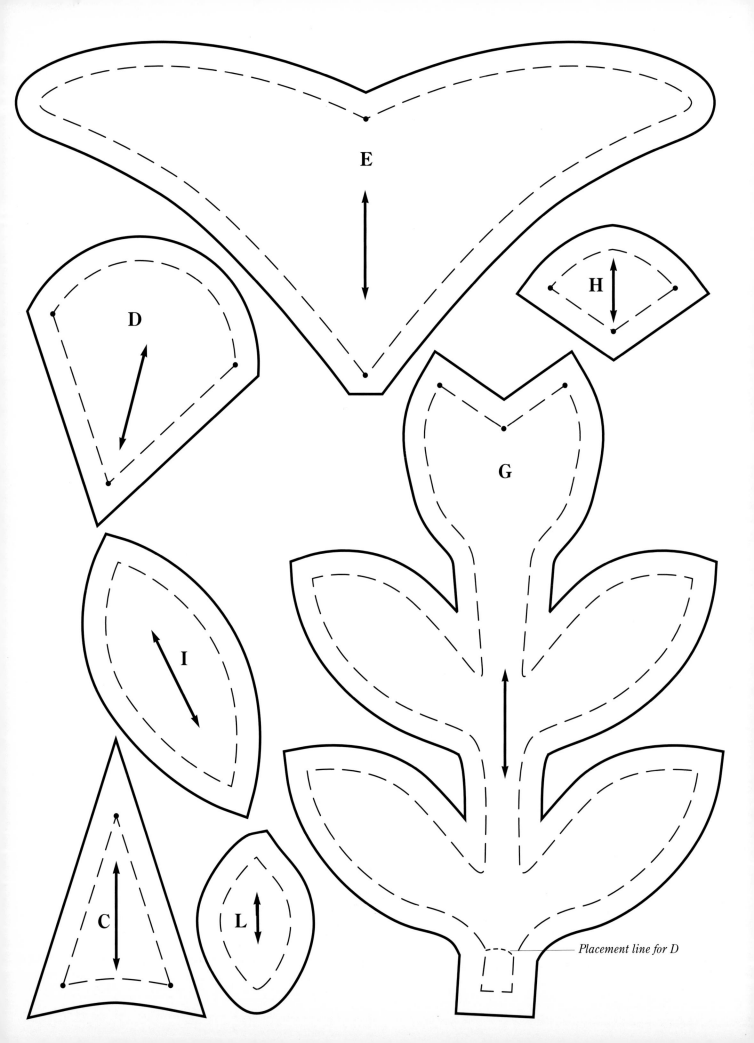

E

D

H

G

I

C

L

Placement line for D

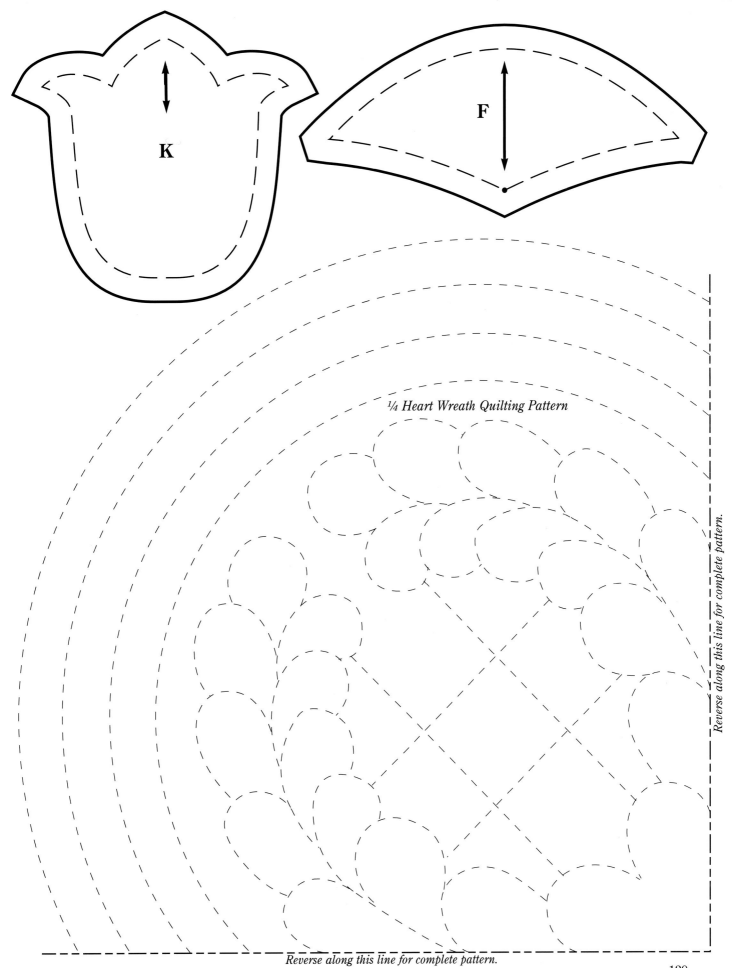

K

F

¼ Heart Wreath Quilting Pattern

Reverse along this line for complete pattern.

Reverse along this line for complete pattern.

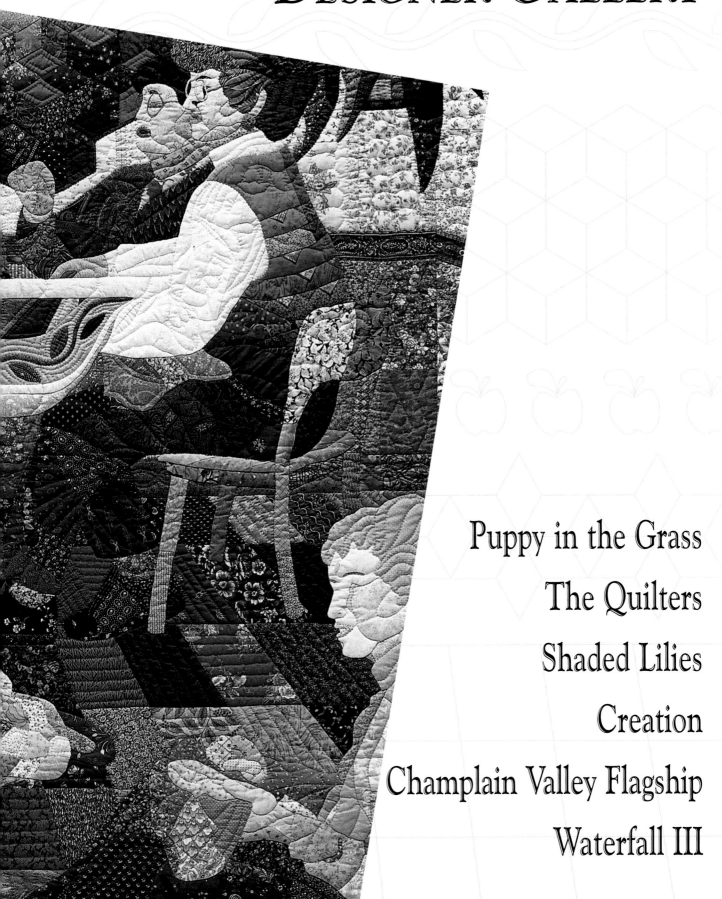

Designer Gallery

"I love all kinds of quilts. I even wear quilts as jackets and vests—after all, I live in Minnesota!"

Sara Newberg King
PINE ISLAND, MINNESOTA

Quiltmaker and teacher Sara King loves to play with fabric. "I often get inspiration for quilts from my fabric," she says. "As I work, I get excited as colors and shapes come together."

Some of her recent pieces have used fabric of her own design. *Shibori Safari,* a jacket, skirt, and hat outfit, makes use of indigo fabric that she has discharge-dyed in a zebra-striped pattern. A wall quilt made from similar fabric is included in the current exhibition "New Quilts From Old Favorites" at the Museum of the American Quilter's Society in Paducah, Kentucky.

Sara has taught quilting in community education classes, in local guilds, and for quilt shops in Minnesota and in Florida. Many of her original quilts have won awards in state and regional shows, and several of her wearable art pieces have appeared in touring exhibitions.

"Everyone has a need to create," Sara says. "I love quilting and enjoy teaching quilting, sharing my enthusiasm with my students."

Puppy in the Grass
1993

In 1993, Sara's daughter Elaine became the proud owner of a puppy she called Bret, who loved to play in the tall grass around the King's country home. "At that time my guild, the Rochester Quilters' Sew-ciety, was sponsoring a challenge," Sara says. "The challenge fabric was a print of leaves, and I decided that it was appropriate to use as a background fabric for the puppy playing in the grass."

Sara cut out and faced some of the leaves from the print, making three-dimensional appliqués for the quilt. (See Quilt Smart on page 133 for technique.) *Puppy in the Grass* won the award for best machine quilting in the 1993 Rochester Quilters' Sew-ciety show.

"I made this quilt for Elaine because Bret is her dog," Sara says. "However, it usually hangs in the kitchen where everyone enjoys it."

❖ Quilt Smart

Faced Appliqué

Sara cut out a leaf motif chosen from the challenge fabric, cutting slightly outside the line of the leaf. From a backing fabric, she cut out a matching shape.

Placing *wrong* sides together, Sara sandwiched the fabrics between two sheets of wash-away stabilizer and pinned the layers together. Threading her machine with metallic thread through the needle and the bobbin, Sara satin-stitched around the edges of the motifs. She then tore away as much stabilizer as possible and removed the remainder by immersing the appliqué in cool water. As a final step, she attached the appliqué by hand to the completed quilt.

"My designs always have a personal feeling," says Marlene Woodfield. "Sometimes it's the locale, or maybe imagery of family or friends."

Marlene has been working with pictorial designs since making her first quilt, a "road map" of Valparaiso University she made in 1976 as a graduation gift for her daughter. She particularly enjoys appliqué and is currently working with designs that require multiple fabrics, like *The Quilters*. "This one is a contemporary charm quilt," she says. "It contains 1,428 different fabrics that I collected from quilt shops all over the Midwest."

Marlene Brown Woodfield
LAPORTE, INDIANA

The Quilters
1994

Marlene conceived the idea for *The Quilters* in 1992, while traveling home with her friends from the National Quilting Association show in Bowling Green, Ohio. "I had received first place in the Scrap Quilt category and a Judge's Recognition award for my wall hanging *The Charm of Impressionism*," Marlene says. "I was wondering what I could do to top that showing."

After deciding to make another charm quilt featuring the nine friends who called themselves the Gourmet Quilters, Marlene began collecting fabrics and taking photographs of the people she would include in the quilt.

"When the quilt was first shown," Marlene says, "I surprised each woman with a button showing her facial image from the quilt and her name. We wear these whenever the quilt is shown, creating quite a stir. My friends claim that the attention they receive from being part of the quilt is better than mine because they didn't have to make it!"

The Quilters are Evelyn Molloy Carpenter, Earlene Burlison Cassidy, Catherine Holland England, Kathryn Phares Gielow, Meredith Stavropoulous Guistrom, Susan Cross Hughes, Dorothy Hardy Sparks, Marlene Brown Woodfield, and Janet Norris Woodruff.

"Sometimes," says Ruby Hall, "it takes a knock on the head to let you know what's really important."

Ten years ago, Ruby, like many other mothers of young children, spent much of her time waiting at the ballpark, carpooling, and dreaming of the day she could move to the country and finally start quilting. Then serious illness struck. "The doctors couldn't tell me if I would live two years or 20," she says quietly. "So I decided that it was time to do what I really wanted to do."

The Halls sold their house in the suburbs, moved a mobile home to a piece of country property they had bought years before, and began to build their dream house. "I bought lots of quilting books and tried everything," she says. "My experience in sewing for the girls came in handy as I taught myself to quilt."

Living with birds, flowers, and the occasional deer in her garden, Ruby credits her lifestyle change with the improvement in her health. "I'm out here next to nature," she says. "The kids are grown now, I'm making quilts, and my doctors say I'm healthy again. I'm just one of the luckiest human beings alive!"

Ruby Hall
VANCE, ALABAMA

Shaded Lilies
1994

Shaded Lilies began with a photograph taken on a summer visit. "My sister had planted red daylilies beside a swing at her home," Ruby says. "One day when I was there, the lilies were in shadow and seemed to stretch toward the sunshine. The colors were fabulous. I went home, got my camera, and started taking pictures and sketching."

About that same time, Ruby's statewide guild, Quilt Alabama, announced plans for a juried exhibition with the theme "Conversations: Sweet Talkin' Sass."

"I wanted to show the lily quilt," Ruby says, "but I couldn't figure out what kind of conversation the flowers were having! It wasn't until the day the show was hung that I finally gave it the temporary name of *Call for the Sunshine.*"

By whatever name, Ruby's quilt received so much attention during the show that she was invited to hang a one-woman exhibition the following spring at Kentuck Museum Gallery in nearby Northport. "I'll be glad when *Lilies* comes home," Ruby says. "It's my grandson's favorite quilt, and he misses the sunshine."